EARLY
MEXICAN·HOUSES

Masonry bench in the entry of a house at Puebla

EARLY MEXICAN·HOUSES

A·BOOK·OF·PHOTOGRAPHS·&·MEASURED·DRAWINGS

BY·G·RICHARD·GARRISON
AND··GEORGE·W·RUSTAY

With a preface to the new edition by David Gebhard

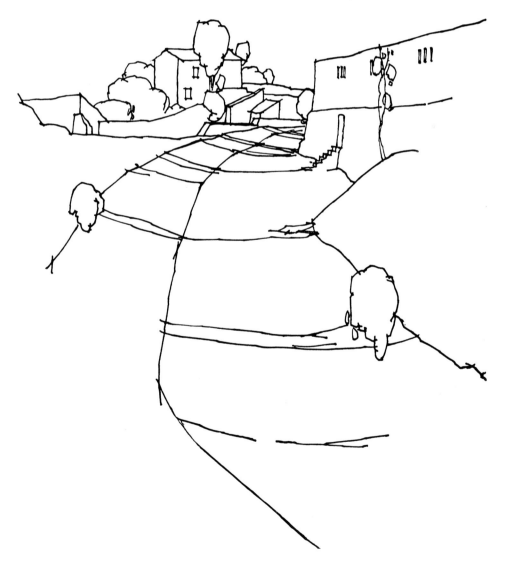

ARCHITECTURAL·BOOK·PUBLISHING·COMPANY·INC

TAYLOR TRADE PUBLISHING

Lanham • New York • Boulder • Toronto • Plymouth, UK

The authors wish to express their grateful appreciation to the people of Mexico for the universal spirit of hospitality and for the sympathetic co-operation with which they were always received, to acknowledge the assistance of all those well informed persons who were the source of much valuable and authentic information, and to thank the Sr. Moisés Sáenz, Sub-secretary of the Secretaría de Educación Pública de Mexico, and the Sr. Jorge Encisco, Jefe de Departamento de Bellas Artes, for the encouragement and facilities which in their official capacities they so courteously accorded them.

Published by Taylor Trade Publishing
An imprint of The Rowman & Littlefield Publishing Group, Inc.
4501 Forbes Boulevard, Suite 200, Lanham, Maryland 20706
www.rlpgtrade.com

Estover Road, Plymouth PL6 7PY, United Kingdom

Distributed by National Book Network

Copyright © 1930, 1990 by Architectural Book Publishing Company
First Taylor Trade Publishing edition 2012

The Architectural Book Publishing Company edition of this book was previously catalogued by the Library of Congress. Catalog Card Number: 90-703

ISBN 978-1-58979-682-9 (pbk. : alk. paper)
ISBN 978-1-58979-683-6 (electronic)

∞™ The paper used in this publication meets the minimum requirements of American National Standard for Information Sciences—Permanence of Paper for Printed Library Materials, ANSI/NISO Z39.48-1992.

Printed in the United States of America

FOREWORD

INCE the beginning of this century, research in the architecture of other countries has produced with increasing frequency the source material available to modern architects and their fellows in the allied arts. If there is truth in the opinion that the development of our architecture will continue to depend partly upon a thorough knowledge of the building of former times, then there may be sufficient reason for presenting books of the nature of this one, in which the authors profess nothing more than to show graphically a few houses of lesser importance built in Mexico during the days of the vice-roys.

Of the tremendous amount of building done in that country between the time of the conquest and the close of the Eighteenth Century, the first place in relative importance must undoubtedly be given to the principal churches, the magnificent old convents, and to the State and private palaces; the most interesting examples of which have already been presented in the works of various authors. Among these, Sylvester Baxter's "Spanish Colonial Architecture in Mexico," published unfortunately in an edition so limited as to be now almost unavailable, is perhaps still the most authoritative. A few weeks of wandering through Mexico in 1925 were sufficient to prove that much interesting and occasionally valuable material of the minor and domestic sort existed, which neither space nor propriety had permitted including among more significant examples in the works of former authors. In planning a visit to Mexico which included ten months in 1928 and 1929, the authors intended deliberately to disregard all buildings of the more monumental and pretentious type, and although it was, of course, impossible not to pause frequently to admire the magnificence of the Churiguresque and the commanding beauty of what Dr. Atl aptly calls the Ultra-Baroque, it was only in this way that time would permit the accumulation of sufficient examples of the other type. Some weeks spent in visiting various sections of the country seemed to show that it might be more sensible to limit the work not only to one class of building but to select only those places most attractive and representative, and, though they be limited to include only a few districts, try to present them with a fair amount of thoroughness.

The opening of the Sixteenth Century saw the land which is now Mexico being added to Spain's already vast Colonial Empire. Successful and prosperous, with her people united and her territory greatly extended, the Mother Country represented at this time what was perhaps the most dominant civilization in Europe. After a brief period of conquest which followed the landing of Hernando Cortez in 1529, her colonists began arriving in New Spain. The culture, the faith, and the customs which these people brought with them were to be, at least in their outward and visible indications, the civilization of the new country.

For centuries before this time, there had existed in Mexico native races not only numerous but highly developed and skillful in the art of building, and in the years that followed, these furnished the craftsman and continued to influence the direction of their country's architecture. In many branches of the arts and sciences these people were the equal, if not, indeed, the superior, of the Europeans. The leaders of their enlightened civilization lived in palaces as luxurious and built on a scale as grand as were those of the European rulers. Although it is not necessary to repeat here the numerous talents and capacities of these people, it is to be noted that they were able to furnish the armies of trained and gifted artisans without whom the enormous amount of building done during the Vice-regal Period could not have been produced.

The violence and dissention of almost continuous revolution which Mexico has suffered since the early Nineteenth Century make it increasingly difficult to realize the wealth and power which were her's during the preceding three centuries of comparative tranquillity. A relatively small group, almost all of whom were either Spanish or of Spanish descent, held title to the lands and controlled the country's almost unlimited resources. The royal fifth from her fabulous mines filled the coffers of the Spanish Exchequer. Those who came to make their fortunes in Mexico were often from the most illustrious, even the most noble families of Spain. A native population held in submission by the force of Spanish arms permitted the development of a caste system, furnished the labor to make possible vast enterprises, and made Mexico in the Eighteenth Century one of the richest countries in the world. The amount of skilled and competent labor to be had at small expense and the abundance of good building material, easy of access, created a volume of permanent building which few countries had equalled. Her great wealth made her a patron of the arts, in which she not only excelled herself, but for her churches and private collections, bought abroad the best works of the masters of other countries. Indeed she is said to have possessed in the Eighteenth Century more gems of the European schools than any other country.

The situation affords a striking contrast with that which existed in our own early colonies, where newcomers often recruited from among the poor, the persecuted, and even the criminal classes struggled for their very existence. Ninety-nine years before the Dutch bought the Island of Manhattan, the present City of Mexico was being rebuilt by the conquerors; a century before the Pilgrim Fathers landed at Plymouth Rock, a school of fine arts taught painting there, and books, music, and wood engravings were being printed on Spanish presses.

In style and character the great buildings of Mexico are a reflection of those of their period in Spain: were built while the province was an important though isolated unit of Spain's empire. Nevertheless, we may, with sufficient reason, refer to the architecture of Mexico as her own. The more important examples of the architecture of most countries are distinguished by a certain similarity: an air of internationalism due, possibly, to the foreign study and travel which it has been the custom to accord to students of the arts, or to the closer contacts which have always existed between the leaders of each country and those of their neighbors. Ever since Greek artists helped build a grander Rome, there have been numerous examples of building done in one country by the architects of another. Peter Charles Lenfant, who was a Frenchman, drew plans for our own National Capital. Much of our colonial architecture was done while this country was British territory; but the buildings of that time we refer to not as English, but as American Colonial architecture.

Although, in a large sense, the old houses of Mexico are similar to those of Spain, natural forces were sufficient to distinguish them from those of the Mother Country. In the buildings of lesser importance, the effect of these influences becomes more noticeable, while the distinguishing features of the borrowed style become less apparent. A necessary adjustment to the wide range of climatic conditions and to the social customs of the new country, the use of local material for building and the employment of native craftsmen, the concessions resulting from a fusion of the Spanish with the Indian Races and their knowledge of Oriental art (gained by an active trade with China which they conducted through the Pacific Port of Acapulco); all these were natural forces which left their stamp even more definitely upon the country's minor and domestic buildings than upon those for the design of which Spanish architects were more directly responsible.

Of the houses in this book, very few are the work of architects. They were done usually by the most expert masons of the town, whose inspiration was drawn indirectly from the more important monuments of the same place. In plan they were adapted sensibly to the requirements of the owner and to the terrain. The character of their ornament depended on the skill of workers, influenced by a background of what, for lack of a better term, we may call the Aztec tradition. These people, who seldom left the place where they were born and whose ancestors came from races differing greatly in temperament and characteristics, were in part responsible for the individual nature of the work of various sections. It is perhaps true to say that in any country it is the architecture of secondary importance which best reflects the life and the people of the time.

"So extensive was the architectural activity in Mexico throughout the historic periods of the Spanish-Colonial occupation, so prolific in results, so general, and—for this continent—so unexampled in its lavish employment of the decorative arts, that it might be easy for a student of its phases to subject himself to the charge of over-enthusiasm, of an overestimate of its qualities. These qualities reside largely in strongly impressive effects,—such as a monumental domination of environment, a union with, and accentuation of, the fascinating elements of landscape and climate, inexhaustibly picturesque and enchantingly spectacular. Classic in fundamental derivation, and possessing marked Oriental attributes, this architecture is freely romantic in its development—often most waywardly so."

Perhaps the most distinguishing feature of the Mexican house is the patio—or interior court—around one or more of which they are generally planned. It is here that the builders have best displayed their ingenuity and their enthusiastic appreciation of the value of form and color in decoration. Screened from public view by high walls, the patio becomes not only the center of family life, but the architectural key around which the house is built. From the street, one passes through a covered entry way to the principal patio, onto which important rooms open directly. Across one or more sides are open corridors, frequently arcaded. Almost invariably there is a fountain either in the center or against a wall, and the place is gay with flowers and trees and bright-colored birds in cages.

In the higher altitudes, patios are more restricted in size and arranged with masonry walls entirely enclosing them. Paved with brick or stone, they capture the warmth of the sun during the day so that the house will be warm and livable during the night. In the tropical and sub-tropical tierra-caliente, they become in general more spacious, often open on one side into a garden or orchard, or are themselves planned and planted so that they become miniature gardens.

The inherent love of flowers has led to the adoption and development of all manner of accessories and details for the arrangement, growth, and protection of plants. Along the tops of walls and balustrades, in the entry ways and around the fountains, are rows of gay mecetas, flower-pots usually of burned clay in an infinite variety of shapes and sizes, each with its separate potted plant. Often to gain additional space for the mecetas, they build against the patio walls and in the corners shelves of masonry, sometimes single and sometimes in tiers receding at various levels. These they call pollos. The patios are shaded sometimes by a fig tree, a bitter-orange, or by other decorative trees of moderate size, around the base of which they build circular boxes of masonry called arreatas, which are for the practical purpose of protecting them from insects, although often they are made in interesting shapes and decorated to be features of the patio. Over one wall the magenta blossoms of a bougianvilla may lend a note of vivid color.

Except on the farms and haciendas and on the outskirts of the cities, isolated houses are uncommon. The streets of urban districts present a line of one or two story facades usually severe and plain except for occasional spots of concentrated ornament. The windows of the first floor are protected by a grille of wood or iron, while those above the street most frequently have balconies, although they, too, are sometimes grilled. It is interesting to observe that both grilles and balcony balustrades on important houses are always of wrought iron, wood being used only on the poorer houses. The balconies are of sufficient width for comfort and their railings are of the proper height to support a person's elbows while leaning. The most dominant and ornamented feature of the facade is the entrance doorway, which, with the entry-way, is called the zaguán and serves as both carriage and pedestrian entrance. A secondary feature is the portón, a grilled gate sometimes of iron, but more often of wood, which separates the patio from the entry-way. It somewhat screens the patio and gives a measure of protection while the great doors of the zaguán stand open during the day —at the same time passers-by are afforded a brief but often fascinating glimpse of a sunlit patio beyond. Another feature at the entrance which typifies in a sense the hospitality of the land is the masonry bench at the entrance. This is placed in the entry-way, or in country places, against the wall outside.

In lower latitudes where rainfall is heaviest the houses have pitched tile roofs, the degree of pitch being determined more or less by the amount of rainfall. In the higher and drier sections of the country flat roofs have developed. Often these are insulated with a foot or more of earth supported on the bricks which span the ceiling beams beneath and paved above the earth with bricks again.

A commendable and ingenious use of material is found throughout the country. In fact, the frankly organic character of the structural work which is allowed to express its functions with all freedom is perhaps the highest merit of the country's architecture. Stone is commonly and extensively used for structural walls and throughout the complete list of architectural details. In places suffering from earthquakes, walls of cut stone were laid up in almost square sizes. Fine walls were made by laying the stone up at random on a very deep bed of mortar into which small bits of stone were pushed to protect against weathering. Walls of mixed masonry are common, and when used are plastered over. Sometimes houses using cut stone trim around doors and windows and for columns and arches have their walls of adobe or of mixed masonry and brick. Carved stone usually shows marked native characteristics due to the fact that the craftsmen had an individual decorative inheritance from the Aztec builders. It is to be noted that the materials used are those which give permanence to building.

Bricks vary in appearance and usage. When used to form walls, columns, arches, balustrades, and mouldings, they are usually plaster covered and the plaster itself may be modeled to give the final form and finish. By themselves, bricks were used for floors and for ceilings where they span between the wooden beams. Molded in unusual shapes, they are used to form graceful citarillas which rail the open corridors and enclose the gardens. Very fine effects are often obtained by a combination of bricks with glazed tiles, used either as a veneer for wall surfaces, solid balustrades and benches, or for floors. Laid above a fill of earth and clay, bricks form the protective covering of flat roofs.

Adobe, which is Mexico's most common and inexpensive building material, is a mixture of mud and straw formed in blocks about four by twelve by twenty-four inches in size and baked in the sun. It is used for building the casas popular or small ranch houses and for the poorer houses of the towns, is inexpensive, easily handled and a marvelous insulator against changes in temperature. When used for walls, it is customary to set them on stone foundations; and when protected with a coating of plaster and copings of paving tile they will stand for centuries.

Plaster, which was used freely on both exterior and interior walls, was made quite hard and weather resisting. In addition to being used as a protective covering, its use has been common for modeled ornament. The 18th Century produced many beautiful walls, friezes, and occasional ceilings of modeled plaster.

What the interiors of the old houses were like in past centuries it is difficult to determine. As they are now, the general impression is one of barrenness—perhaps they would always have seemed so to visitors from the North. Ceilings were almost universally of wood beams, spanned by large paving bricks. Both beams and bricks were always exposed and often decorated with painted designs in various colors. The beams were carried on a plain molded wood sill, above a painted or frescoed frieze. In certain sections, wooden boards were used instead of bricks above the beams. Occasionally the entry way and corridors had vaulted ceilings. Sometimes rooms had a dado of glazed tiles but more often it was simply a flat painted band, as were the trims around the openings. Above the deep splayed doors and windows the conchas, as they were called—for their shape was roughly that of the inside of a shell, often became the most elaborate features of the rooms, being treated in innumerable ways in modeled plaster.

Glazed tile in an infinite variety of colors and applications forms the distinguishing feature of the buildings in certain districts. When used by itself, it presents its most interesting and colorful effects. In this manner it is used for floors, wainscots, and niches for lavabos, which are wash basins, as well as for ceilings and the balustrades of stairways. Probably the most distinctive tiles are the blue and white azulejos of Puebla, for which that city has been famous since the early 17th Century; but from other districts come tiles of various rich and harmonious colors equally as beautiful.

The use of wood, which was seldom found in great quantities, was confined largely to structural beams and columns, doors and solid paneled windows, turned grilles and balustrades. Very infrequently, it was used for the trim of doors and windows, for plank floors, and wooden ceilings. The authors found houses entirely constructed of wood only in one district.

In the use of iron and bronze the old craftsmen were particularly adept, some towns and villages being veritable museums of fine lock-shields, door pulls, hinges, and other hardware. Wrought iron grilles and balconies of excellent workmanship are found in abundance. It was customary for the larger and more important houses to have their grilles of iron, while the use of wood for these features was limited to houses of lesser importance.

A feature in all parts of Mexico is the unrestrained use of color with which effects are more often gained by the free use of water paint than by the natural color of the materials. Exteriors are painted usually once a year and it is the accumulation of various shades and colors from several seasons which make the wall surfaces look so rich and pleasing. Often houses are free of all ornament and moldings, the relief and effect being obtained by the use of broad painted bands which trim the door and window openings or do duty as a cornice to finish off the tops of wall areas. The body of the wall is painted another shade as are the dados, which are usually much darker.

The brick paved floors of rooms and corridors are stained weekly with cochineal. An important item about the use of color is that it was almost always in soft grayed shades and applied in flat tones, the variation in color coming through the natural effects of weathering. Very seldom was color used in a pure or raw state, and for this reason the houses of towns which are highly colorful are neither gaudy nor ostentatious.

In these brief notes we have not attempted to describe completely the many interesting features which distinguish the houses of Mexico, but rather to sum up in a general way a few of the common characteristics more clearly shown in the photographs and drawings which follow.

G. Richard Garrison
George W. Rustay

PREFACE TO THE NEW EDITION

by DAVID GEBHARD

FOR well over a century the architecture, landscape architecture, and art of Mexico have held a fascination for those of us living in the United States. The duration and intensity of this interest is reflected in a striking succession of borrowing which has taken place for close to one hundred years. The first of these, which came about in the years 1900 through the 1920s, looked to the churches and public buildings of Mexico. The high point of this inspirational borrowing was the 1915 Panama California International Exposition in San Diego, designed by Bertram G. Goodhue and his associates.

Concurrent with this interest in Spanish Colonial architecture was the romantic attraction of the region's Pre-Columbian art and architecture. The potential of this native American art and architecture as a potent source for contemporary design entered the scene in the 1890s, resulting in a fascinating chapter in American architecture, peopled by such diverse personages as Frank Lloyd Wright, Alfred C. Bossom, and Robert Stacy-Judd.

Yet another arena of interchange was in city planning. It was the architectural critic, Montgomery Schuyler, who suggested in 1912, that the advocates of the City Beautiful movement in this country could learn much from the centuries of Mexican experiences in city planning. "Everywhere," he wrote, "you find in the Spanish settlements the civic centre or central plaza, everywhere the 'Alameda,' or public garden and place of recreation. All of this ought to instruct while it shames us".[1]

Contemporaneous with these affairs, and continuing on into the early 1930s, was the allure of the Mexican house, its patio and garden. Then, following in the thirties, was the deep and lasting impact of the great Mexican muralists, which served as an inspiration for so much of the W.P.A. mural art of these years. Finally, there was the Post World War II affair of Mexican Modernist architecture, which so pointedly encouraged American architects to abstract, enrich and romanticize the International Style.

American architects had their first introduction into the Spanish Colonial architecture of Mexico via two long series of articles published in the *American Architect* in the 1880s and early 1890s. The first of these was by the Boston savant, Sylvester Baxter, who since the early 1880s had spent a number of years living and traveling throughout Mexico.[2] In his series of sixteen articles under the title, "Strolls About Mexico", published between 1883 and 1892, he provided vivid descriptions of churches, gardens and houses, often accompanied by delightful small sketches.[3]

During the years that the Baxter articles were appearing, a similar series on Mexico was run in the same magazine, authored by Arthur Howard Noll.[4] Like Baxter, Noll captured the spirit of this architecture in his text and accompanying drawings, helping in part to set the stage for such later North American transplants as the San Diego Exposition. Noll's 1888 portrait of the Spanish Colonial architecture of the city of Jalapa could just as well have been transplanted to 1915 and used as the description of the buildings and gardens of the San Diego Exposition: "In the town itself the spotless white of the buildings is relieved by the brilliant green of the graceful tropical foliage. Over each white wall hangs a banana leaf. From each enclosed tower, a coconut palm. The buildings present an almost endless variety of form. Every picturesque feature of architecture is to be found; buttresses, flying buttresses, oriels, arches, towers, turrets, pinnacles, domes,—all in artistic confusion."[5]

From the early nineteen-hundreds on there was a steady flow of articles and books devoted to the architecture of Mexico, as well as a number of popular guidebooks.[6] Of these the most luxurious by far was Sylvester Baxter's 1901 *Spanish Colonial Architecture in Mexico*, with drawings provided by Bertram G. Goodhue, and photographs by Henry Greenwood Peabody.[7] Baxter's beautifully printed production, (ala William Morris and the Kelmscott Press), consisted of a text volume, accompanied by nine volumes of boxed, mounted prints. It was expensive when published, was limited to five hundred copies, and was therefore not available to a very wide audience of architects and others. None-the-less, it remained as *the* most often cited source book for illustrations and drawings of the principle monuments of Mexican architecture, dating from the 16th through the 18th century.

Though Baxter's friend and colleague, Bertram G. Goodhue, realized many fragments of his even earlier 1892 *Mexican Memories* in his buildings for the San Diego Exposition, he accompanied these with equally intense memories brought back from his travels in Spain, Italy and far off Iran (Persia).[8] As the Mediterranean and Spanish Colonial revival developed in the later teens and on into the 1920s, there was a tendency upon the part of architects and their clients to turn increasingly to Spain and Italy, rather than Mexico, for inspiration. The reasons for this were complex, but in part it had to do with the desire to travel in Europe rather than in neighboring Mexico, and also to the general lack of available articles and books on Mexican architecture, especially those presenting domestic architecture.[9]

As the Spanish Colonial revival shifted ground in the mid-twenties, from the romantic towered and turreted miniaturized castle, to the image of the rural ranch house and Monterey-inspired dwelling, this shift in imagery was accompanied by a growing number of books and articles which were devoted not only to the major buildings of Mexico, but increasingly to its smaller rural and urban houses.

The most important of the books were all published by architects who had visited Mexico and had recorded their experiences almost exclusively via the camera. The British born, New York architect Alfred C. Bossum, in his 1924 *An Architectural Pilgrimage in Old Mexico*, accompanied his photographs with a brief text, and a few sketches.[10] A similar approach was carried out during the following two years in Louis La Beaume's and William Booth Papin's *The Picturesque Architecture of Mexico* (1925); in Atlee B. Ayres' *Mexican Architecture: Domestic, Civil and Ecclesiastical* (1926); and in Garrett Van Pelt's *Old Architecture of Southern Mexico* (1926).[11]

While these volumes were all quarto in size and had large photographs, what they lacked were drawings, and above all measured drawings. While America's Beaux Arts trained architects had developed a remarkable ability to creatively use reproductions and photographs in the design process, nothing could really replace the world of drawings. To address this problem two young architectural draftsmen, George Richard Garrison and George W. Rustay, set out in 1925, and again in 1928 and 1929 to record a select number of examples of the "minor domestic architecture" of Mexico. They divided their labors, with Garrison doing the photographs, and Rustay, the drawings.

Their approach was to fully record a select, limited number of individual buildings through a mixed presentation of photographs, perspective drawings, elevations, floor plans, and details. Such an approach would, they felt, make their projected book quite different from those previously published; it would be a highly useful tool for architects designing Hispanic buildings, and the photographs and drawings were engaging enough to be of interest to the lay public. Though the authors were obviously attached to principle ". . . that the development of our architecture will continue to depend partially upon a thorough knowledge of the buildings of former times. . . ," they presented this argument for traditionalism via perspective drawings which were openly "modern" in style of deliniation.[12] Following suit, the publisher packaged the volume in a modernist manner, employing a striking, "primitive" textile pattern for the end sheets, and contemporary type faces for the cover and for the pages of the book.

As a prelude to the publication of the book a small selection of Garrison and Rustay's photographs and drawings were presented in the November, 1929, issue of the *Architectural Record*.[13] The book itself was published the following year, certainly not the most auspicious moment with the deepening gloom of the Great Depression clouding the scene. William P. Spratling, in reviewing the volume for *Architectural Forum* in 1932, wrote, "The result is a significant work . . . It is full of all sorts of things not taught in architectural schools; . . . It will be a vast surprise to all those urban architects trained in the importance of the masters and the architecturally historic monuments."[14]

Spratling's poignant observations about what architects and others could gain from this book are certainly as relevant for architects today, as they were when written some sixty years ago.

NOTES

1. Montgomery Schuyler, "The Architecture of Mexico City," *Architectural Record* 32 (September 1912: 215).

2. Sylvester Baxter (1850–1927) wrote on a wide array of subjects ranging from urban and regional planning and parks, to articles on New England, the American Southwest, on Walt Whitman, plus publishing his own poetry. Some biographical information concerning his early trips to Mexico are to be found in the last two sections of his series of articles, "Strolls About Mexico," *American Architect* 37 (July 23, 1893: 54–56; and September 3, 1893: 146–147).

3. Sylvester Baxter, "Strolls About Mexico," *American Architect* 14 (October 6, 1883: 159–160); 14 (December 8, 1883: 267–268); 16 (August 16, 1884: 77–78); 17 (February 7, 1885: 63–64); 17 (April 18, 1885: 183); 18 (August 15, 1885: 76–78); 18 (September 19, 1885: 135–136); 18 (October 31, 1885: 207–208); 19 (January 9, 1886: 15–17); 19 (February 13, 1886: 78–79); 19 (March 18, 1886: 123–124); 19 (June 12, 1886: 283–285); 20 (August 21, 1886: 83–84); 35 (January 16, 1892: 41–43); 37 (July 23, 1892: 54–56); 37 (September 3, 1892: 146–147).

4. Arthur Howard Noll, "Autumn Journeys in Mexico," *American Architect* 23 (June 30, 1888: 305–306); 24 (October 13, 1888: 172–173); 24 (December 22, 1888: 287–288); 24 (December 29, 1888: 299); 25 (June 15, 1889: 282–283); 25 (June 29, 1889: 305–306).

5. Arthur Howard Noll, "Autumn Journeys in Mexico," *American Architect* 24 (December 22, 1888: 287).

6. Amoung these would be Ralph W. Emerson, *The Architecture and Furniture of the Spanish Colonies During the 17th and 18th Centuries Including Mexico, Cuba, Porto Rico and the Philippenes.* (Boston: Geo. H. Polley & Co., 1901); Mrs. J. K. Hudson, "The Patio in Mexico," *House and Garden* 4 (July 1903: 41–46); "Spanish Churches in Mexico," *The Brocure*

Series 6 (June 1901); F.F. McArthur, "Views in Old Mexico," *American Architect* 96 (December 1, 1909); Sherril Schell, "The Mexican Patio," *American Architect* 95 (November 10, 1909: 181–183); Marrion Wilcox, "Certain Phases on Spanish Colonial Architecture," *Architectural Record* 37 (June 1915: 535–546).

7. Sylvester Baxter, *Spanish Colonial Architecture of Mexico* 10 vols. (Boston: J. B. Millet, 1901); another limited edition was published in the same year by the Boston firm of G. M. Allen Co.

8. Bertram G. Goodhue, "Of Persian Gardens," *Century* 73 (March 1907: 739–48); Bertram G. Goodhue, *A Book of Architectural and Decorative Drawings* (New York: Architectural Book Publishing Co., 1914).

9. Characteristic of writings on Mexican architecture after the First World War would be the articles by Walter H. Kilham ["Impressions of the Colonial Architecture of Mexico," *Architectural Forum* 34 (January 1921: 39–44; 7 March 1921: 85–90); "Mexican Renaissance," *Architectural Forum* 37 (November 1922: 209–214); 38 (January 1923: 1–6)]; William S. Spratling, "Some Impressions of Mexico," *Architectural Forum* 47 (July 1927: 1–7), 47 (August 1927: 161–168).

10. Alfred C. Bossoms, *An Architectural Pilgrimage in Old Mexico.* (New York: Scribner's Sons, 1923).

11. Louis la Beaume and William Booth Papin, *The Picturesque Architecture of Mexico.* (New York: The Architectural Book Publishing Co., 1925); Atlee B. Ayres, *Mexican Architecture: Domestic, Civil and Ecclesiastical.* (New York: Wm. Helburn, 1926); Garrett Van Pelt, Jr., *Old Architecture of Southern Mexico* (Cleveland: J. H. Jensen, 1926).

12. George Richard Garrison and George W. Rustay, *Mexican Houses* (New York: Architectural Book Publishing Co., 1930: VII).

13. George Richard Garrison and George W. Rustay, "Portfolio of Mexican Minor Architecture," *Architectural Record* 66 (November 1929: 540–549).

14. "Book Department: Domestic Architecture in Mexico, a review by William P. Spratling, *Architectural Forum* 54 (January, 1931: 26–27). The architect, William P. Spratling, had himself traveled extensively in Mexico, and had published a group of his drawings in the *Architectural Forum* in 1927 (see note #9). Spratling's style of rendering conveyed a modernist quality similar to that of Rustay.

LIST OF PLATES

LIST OF PLATES—*Concluded*

All photographs and measured drawings reproduced in this book
are the original work of the authors, and are the result of research for which they were commissioned by the Secretaría de
Educación Pública de Mexico.

PUEBLA
1929
GEO.WIRLOSTDY

The fountain at Santa Rosa

FOUNDED in 1532 by order of the Audiencia Real, a new city known as Puebla was built where the Sierra Madre Range slopes gently to the floor of the great valley, and at some distance south and west from the Capital. Almost immediately it took its place as one of the most important centers of the country, occasionally rivalling even the City of Mexico. Since the middle of the seventeenth century it has been the home of Mexico's glazed tile industry and makes free use of the brilliant colored azulejos in all classes of buildings. The casa de altas or two-story house predominates. Though structural walls are almost always of stone they are frequently faced on the exterior with flat brick, either alone or with glazed tile inserts, and laid up in herringbone and other ingenious patterns, usually in large panels separated by stone belt courses and wide-spaced pilasters of stone. The bricks are usually painted a light color with water paint. Many of the older houses present an appearance almost medieval with their ponderous walls and heavy second floor patio corridors supported on arches swung over massive stone corbels, relieved, however, by a free but excellent use of color and by an occasional fig tree or the magenta blossoms of a bougainvillea whose broken shadows decorate the wall and give a garden look of coolness.

Arcaded side of patio in an early Eighteenth Century House. Columns of stone, walls of mixed masonry, plastered over. A single fig tree with its shadows softens the light and contrasts with the salmon pink painted walls

Patio of a house on the Plaza de San Miguel. The plastered walls are painted with water paint, a rich yellow ochre, and trimmed with a warm grey. A scarlet blooming bougainvillea covers the far wall. Part of a round stone corner fountain shows in the foreground

The arched entrance at San Antonio. The wall recently painted yellow, has scaled off in patches, showing grey blue and rose paint of former seasons. The tile trimmed door beyond leads to a garden patio

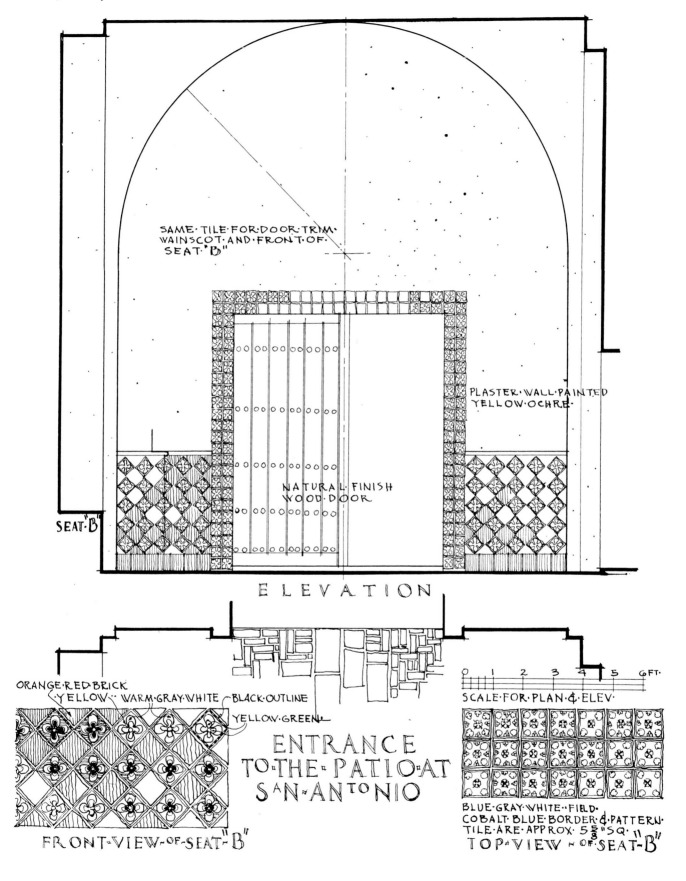

SAME · TILE · FOR · DOOR · TRIM ·
WAINSCOT · AND · FRONT · OF ·
SEAT · "B"

PLASTER · WALL · PAINTED
YELLOW · OCHRE ·

NATURAL · FINISH
WOOD · DOOR

SEAT · "B"

E L E V A T I O N

ORANGE · RED · BRICK
YELLOW · · WARM · GRAY · WHITE · · BLACK · OUTLINE
YELLOW · GREEN

SCALE · FOR · PLAN · & · ELEV ·

ENTRANCE
TO · THE · PATIO · AT
SAN · ANTONIO

BLUE · GRAY · WHITE · FIELD ·
COBALT · BLUE · BORDER · & · PATTERN ·
TILE · ARE · APPROX · 5⅝" SQ · "

FRONT · VIEW · OF · SEAT · "B"

TOP · VIEW · OF · SEAT · "B"

Exterior wall treatment showing blue and white tile and brick veneer over a masonry wall. Brick are painted cream white with a water paint

Wall treatment in entry way of a dwelling. Wall is of masonry with orange red brick and blue and white tile veneer. The large square brick are ten and a half, by ten and a half, by two inches

The Vecindad of San Antonio. View of the principal patio from the entry. A vecindad is a dwelling occupied by several families of the working class

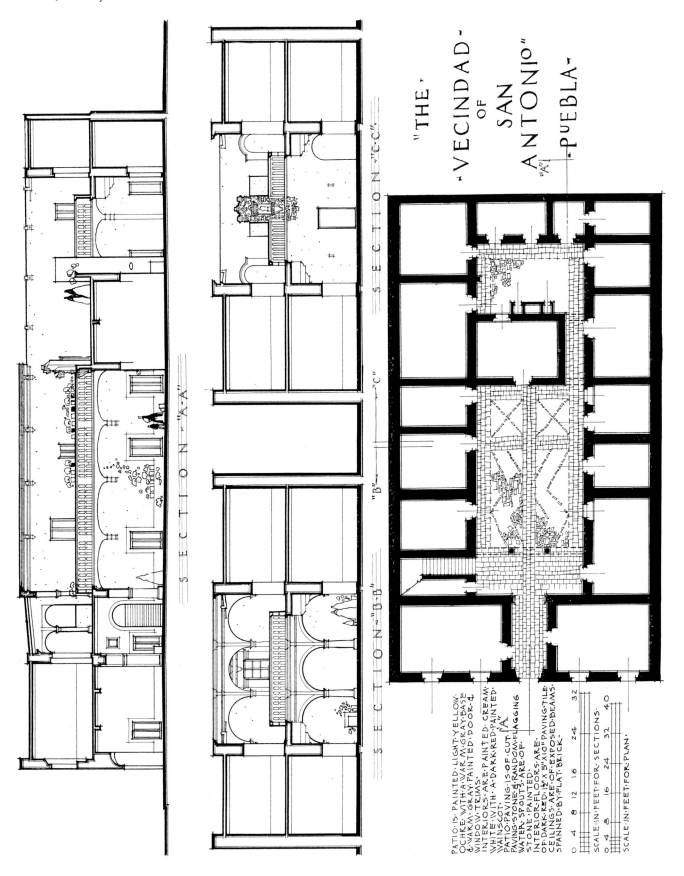

SECTION·"A·A"

SECTION·"B·B"

SECTION·"C·C"

"THE·
·VECINDAD·
OF
SAN·
ANTONIO"
·PUEBLA·

PATIO·IS·PAINTED·LIGHT·YELLOW·
OCHRE·WITH·A·WARM·GRAY·BASE
&·WARM·GRAY·PAINTED·DOOR·&
WINDOW·TRIMS·
INTERIORS·ARE·PAINTED·CREAM·
WHITE·WITH·A·DARK·RED·PAINTED·
WAINSCOT·
PATIO·PAVING·IS·OF·CUT·
PAVING·STONE·&·RANDOM·FLAGGING
WATER·SPOUTS·ARE·OF·
STONE·PAINTED·
INTERIOR·FLOORS·ARE·
OF·DARK·RED·4"X·5"X10"·PAVING·TILE·
CEILINGS·ARE·OF·EXPOSED·BEAMS·
SPANNED·BY·FLAT·BRICK·

0 4 8 12 16   24   32
SCALE·IN·FEET·FOR·SECTIONS·

0 4 8   16   24   32   40
SCALE·IN·FEET·FOR·PLAN·

Puebla, State of Puebla

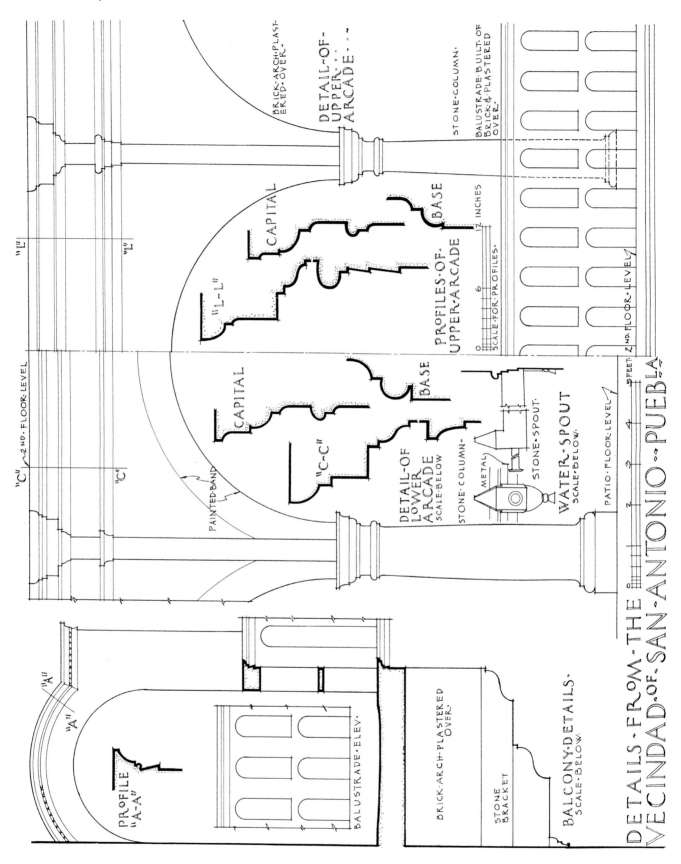

DETAILS·FROM·THE
VECINDAD·OF·SAN·ANTONIO~PUEBLA

10

The Vecindad San Antonio. View of the principal patio toward the entry showing corridor arcaded on two floors

The Vecindad of San Antonio. The niche holds a small painted stone figure of San Antonio, which, with the surrounding enrichment, is the one spot of decoration in an otherwise simple patio

CROSS·MISSING
FIGURE·MISSING

NICHE·IS·BUILT·UP·OF·BRICK
PLASTERED·OVER·&·PAINTED·
MOULDS·ARE·BLOCKED·OUT·
IN·BRICK·&·THEN·RUN·IN·PLASTER·
SAINT·IN·NICHE·SCULPTURED·
STONE·PAINTED·

NICHE
FROM·THE
VECINDAD OF·SAN·ANTONIO··PUEBLA

·SCALE·IN·FEET·

Puebla, State of Puebla

Smoke vent over a kitchen. The bricks are two by five by eleven inches

A carved stone newel post in the patio of a Seventeenth Century dwelling

Puebla, State of Puebla

A stone corbeled balcony with arches of brick plastered over. Shows wrought iron rail with arched braces to the wall, and baskets for flower pots

A bow grilled window of wrought iron. Thin paving brick support the plastered hood. Sill is brick paved. Vertical rods are five-eighths inches square

Vecindad on the Calle del Puente de Analco. View into the patio from the entry. The arched wall is not straight but swings to the right across the normal axis of the view

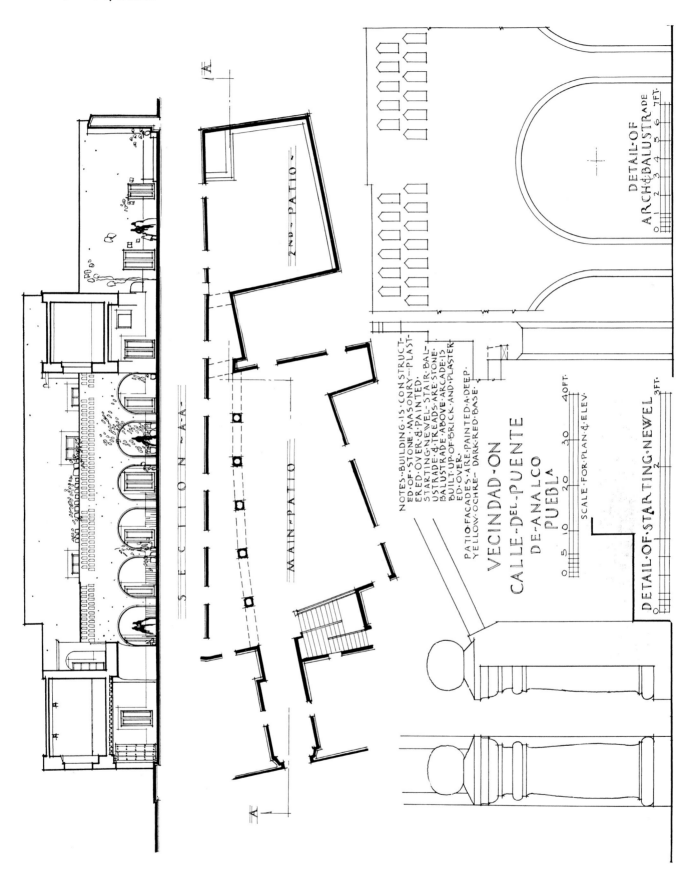

SECTION·A·A

2·ND·PATIO

MAIN·PATIO

A

A

DETAIL·OF·ARCH·&·BALUSTRADE

0 1 2 3 4 5 6 7 FT.

NOTES·BUILDING·IS·CONSTRUCT-
ED·OF·STONE·MASONRY—PLAST-
ERED·OVER·&·PAINTED·
STARTING·NEWEL·STAIR·BAL-
USTRADE·&·TREADS·ARE·STONE·
BALUSTRADE·ABOVE·ARCADE·IS·
BUILT·UP·OF·BRICK·AND·PLASTER-
ED·OVER·
PATIO·FACADES·ARE·PAINTED·A·DEEP·
YELLOW·OCHRE—DARK·RED·BASE·

VECINDAD·ON
CALLE·DEL·PUENTE
DE·ANALCO
PUEBLA

0 5 10 20 30 40 FT.

SCALE·FOR·PLAN·&·ELEV·

DETAIL·OF·STARTING·NEWEL

0 1 2 3 FT.

17

Solid wood doors and elliptical wood grilled transom in the second floor corridor at the head of a stairway. The ornamental center piece is missing from the transom

A small patio seen from the entry. The open stone stair has treads and risers of stone. Railing is of brick, plastered over and painted

Puebla, State of Puebla

A cream pink painted patio typical of many of the older houses of Puebla. The stairway, which lands over the arched entrance from the street, serves only the front portion of the house

A shallow fountain of glazed tile in the patio of a dwelling. The decorated azulejos which line the basin and cover the outside wall are blue and white. The plain ones on top are canary yellow

Puebla, State of Puebla

Street facade of the Casa Fernandez, a seventeenth century house. The long balcony is called a balcon corrida, and occurs frequently in Puebla. The owner's offices and servants' quarters occupy the ground floor, the family the floor above

22

Puebla, State of Puebla

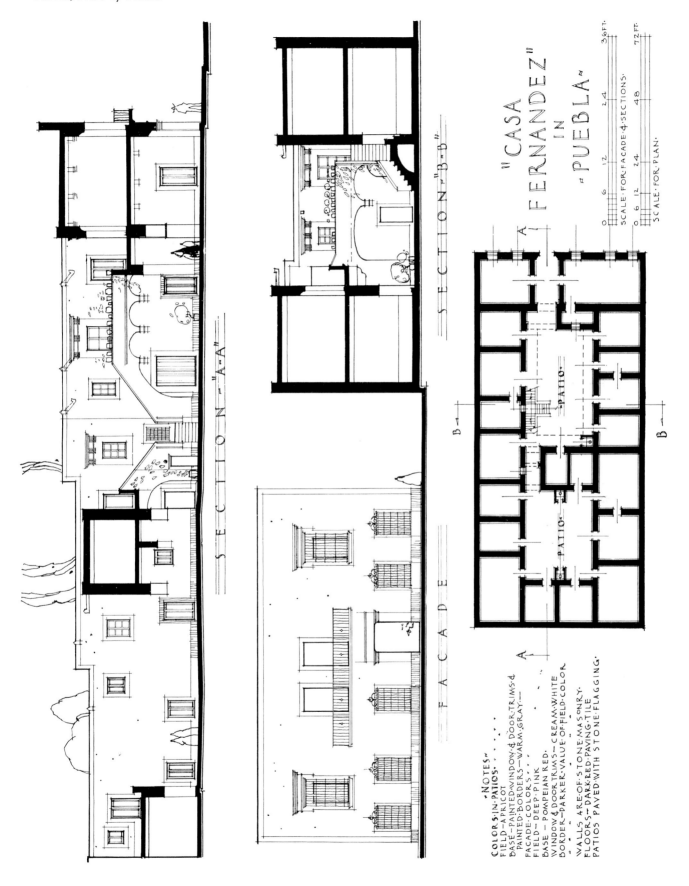

S E C T I O N · "A-A"

S E C T I O N · "B-B"

F A C A D E

"CASA
FERNANDEZ"
IN
"PUEBLA"

SCALE·FOR·FACADE·4·SECTIONS.

SCALE·FOR·PLAN.

"PATIO"

"PATIO"

· "NOTES" ·
·COLORS·IN·PATIOS· · · · ·
FIELD—APRICOT
BASE—PAINTED·WINDOW·&·DOOR·TRIMS·&
PAINTED·BORDERS—WARM·GRAY.—
·FACADE·COLORS· · · ·
FIELD—DEEP·PINK
BASE—POMPEIAN·RED.
WINDOW·&·DOOR·TRIMS—CREAM·WHITE
BORDER—DARKER·VALUE·OF·FIELD·COLOR

WALLS·ARE·OF·STONE·MASONRY.
FLOORS—DARK·RED·PAVING·TILE
PATIOS·PAVED·WITH·STONE·FLAGGING.

23

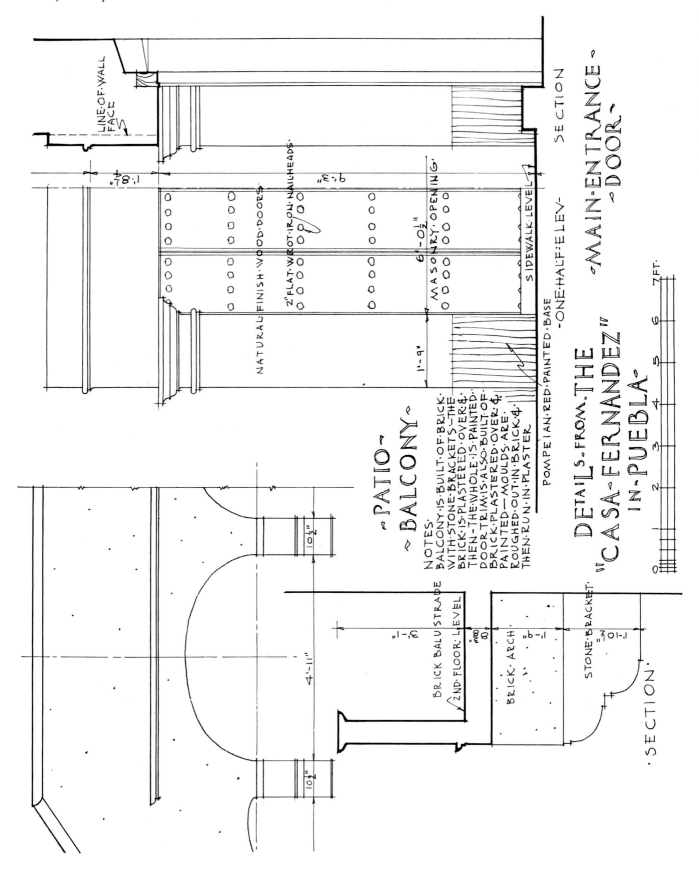

·PATIO·
·BALCONY·

LINE·OF·WALL
FACE

1'-8¾"

NATURAL·FINISH·WOOD·DOORS·

2"·FLAT·WROT·IRON·NAILHEADS·

9'-3"

6'-0½"

MASONRY·OPENING·

SIDE·WALK·LEVEL·

1'-9"

·SECTION·

·ONE·HALF·ELEV·

POMPEIAN·RED·PAINTED·BASE·

·MAIN·ENTRANCE·
·DOOR·

NOTES:
BALCONY·IS·BUILT·OF·BRICK·
WITH·STONE·BRACKETS·THE·
BRICK·IS·PLASTERED·OVER·&·
THEN·THE·WHOLE·IS·PAINTED·
DOOR·TRIM·IS·ALSO·BUILT·OF·
BRICK·PLASTERED·OVER·&·
PAINTED·MOULDS·ARE·
ROUGHED·OUT·IN·BRICK·&·
THEN·RUN·IN·PLASTER

·DETAILS·FROM·THE·
·"CASA·FERNANDEZ"·
·IN·PUEBLA·

0 1 2 3 4 5 6 7 FT.

10½"

4'-11"

10½"

BRICK·BALUSTRADE

2ND·FLOOR·LEVEL

8"-3"

BRICK·ARCH·

1'-9"

STONE·BRACKET·

1'-10"

·SECTION·

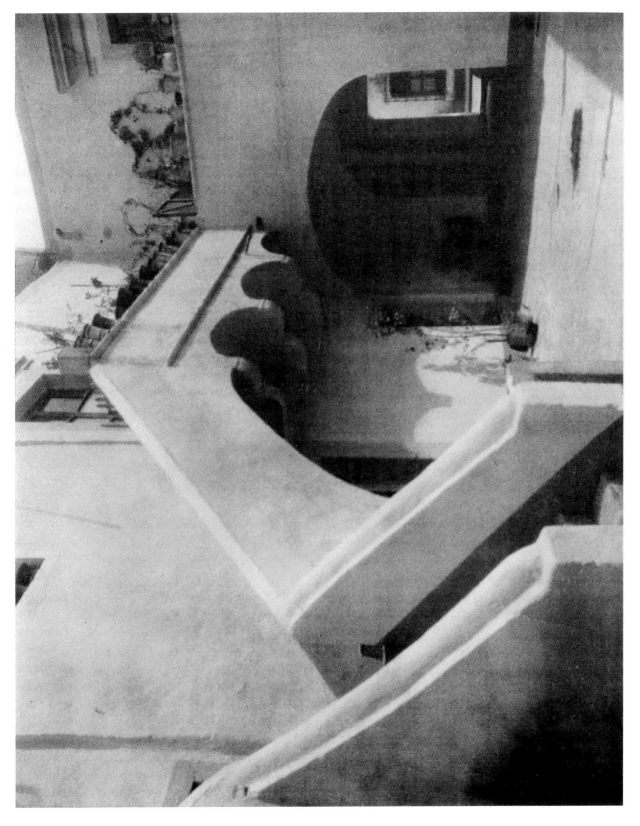

The patio of the Casa Fernandez, a view toward the street. The corridor extends around three sides, and on the fourth drops down to form a double stairway

Puebla, State of Puebla

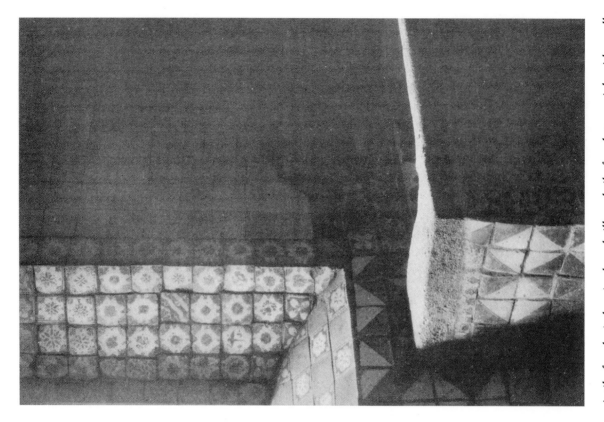

A tile faced window jamb and sill, and tile faced stone sink with small niche above in the kitchen of Santa Rosa

The kitchen of Santa Rosa. The decorated tiles of the architrave are blue and white, the star above, yellow and green

The glazed tile kitchen of Santa Rosa. The field areas are grey white, decorated bands and wainscot are blue and white, architraves are blue, yellow, and white. The new floor is a poor example. The bond of old ones never allowed the pattern to separate into units

Entrance to a dwelling. The entry is three steps below the sidewalk level. The trim of the door and window is of cut stone in a plastered masonry wall. The off center window is not unusual

A masonry wall faced with brick laid in a herringbone pattern, and painted a cream pink with water paint. The stone base is oil painted a light plum brown

Above. A patio arcaded on one side. The flat balusters of the open corridor above are of mixed masonry plastered over. *Below.* A corner of the garden patio at San Antonio. The glazed tile of the wainscot are blue and white. Paving brick with glazed tile inserts face the inside of the solid masonry corridor railing

The Casa Furlong. The unusually high corridor of the living floor permits the entre suelo or in between floor. It is supported across the front and left sides by open arches. Columns and caps are of cut stone. Walls and arches of masonry plastered over and painted mottled yellow with cream trim

OAXACA
1929
GEO·W·RUSTAY

Typical entry of a dwelling

BY the same decree which made Hernando Cortez Marquis of the Valley of Oaxaco, Charles the fifth made a former Indian town with its newcome Castillian families a cuidad in 1529. The buildings of Oaxaca, constructed to resist the frequent earthquakes common to the valley, are low and massive. In the principal plaza the arches of the portales are unusually short and heavy. Cornices and mouldings are simple, their projections slight, and their scale large. Of the houses, the one-story casa baja is the most representative. A unique feature of many of these is the hooded door and window formed by allowing beams imbedded in the wall to project beyond and form a shelter. Various forms may be traced to the Spanish style called Mudejar. The use of wrought iron for grille and barandal is frequent and of excellent workmanship. Often a light portón of wood secures the privacy of the patio while the great doors of the zaguan stand open through the day

Above. Typical second floor corner balcony of wrought iron. Huge wrought flowers like the one on the corner brace are peculiar to Oaxaca and recall the massiveness of the architecture. *Below.* Typical two-window balcon corrido with wrought iron rail and braces which carry the balcony floor beyond the projection of the stone

View of the patio of a dwelling through an entrance arch showing Moorish influence

Facade of a house on the Plaza de la Sangre de Cristo. The drawing opposite is of the ground floor window. Walls are of masonry, plastered and painted a cream yellow with water paint

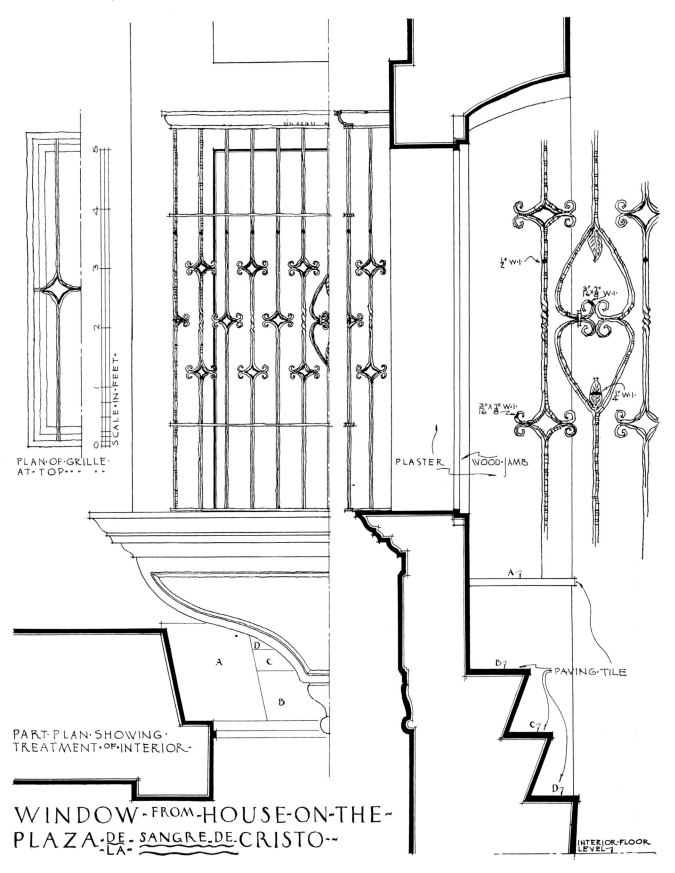

PLAN·OF·GRILLE·
AT·TOP·· · ·

SCALE·IN·FEET·

PLASTER   WOOD·JAMB

½" W·I·

3/16" X 7/8" W·I·

¼" W·I·

3/16" X 7/8" W·I·

A

B

PAVING·TILE

C

D

PART·PLAN·SHOWING·
TREATMENT·OF·INTERIOR·

INTERIOR·FLOOR
LEVEL·

WINDOW·FROM·HOUSE·ON·THE·
PLAZA·DE·SANGRE·DE·CRISTO·~
~LA~

Detail of the ground floor window of the house on the Plaza de la Sangre de Cristo. The wrought metal cornice is typical of the window grilles of Oaxaca

Wood grilled window of a simple one-story house, showing hood of shaped wood beams covered with thin brick and plaster

Wood porton in the entry of a dwelling

Smoke vent on the roof of a casa popular

Facade of a casa baja or one-story house with window grilles of wrought iron. Built up masonry sills are common to the town

A well head of plastered adobe blocks

Detail of a plastered masonry chimney

Facade of the house of the Senorita Diburcia, which has a saint's niche to one side of the doorway

A street scene

ORIGINALLY the capital city of an Indian province, Cuernavaca was one of thirty cities included in the vast lands granted Cortez by the king of Spain. Located on protected southern slopes, the air is notably soft, the climate semi-tropical. Beneath its winding stone paved streets rush numerous mountain streams to water the gardens and orchards with which the town abounds. Along walks shaded by mango trees and flowering orleanders the houses present their painted facades in the usual unbroken line, but on the inside frequently abandon the patio for an open plan with generous corridors which open on to high-walled old gardens. Free use is made of various shaped bricks for garden walls and corridor railings. Although most of the houses are of mixed stone and mortar, some are of adobe and all are plastered and painted. There is rarely a house but has at least one fountain and a myriad of mesetas, each with its separate potted plant. The bougainvillea lends a note of vivid color where it climbs about the house or spreads its blossoms at the top of some stately cedro.

View through the entrance of a small house. An open corridor with exposed tile roof faces the garden. The plain round columns are of mixed masonry plastered and painted white, and capped with thin paving brick

Patio in the Hotel Buena Vista. View of the second floor corridor across one end. Ceiling and walls are painted a cream white, the dado a light blue. The floor is paved with large bricks stained an orange red

Patio in the Hotel Buena Vista. Chamber door at a corner of the second floor corridor. The native chair is green with slats decorated in canary yellow, and turnings on the legs painted gold

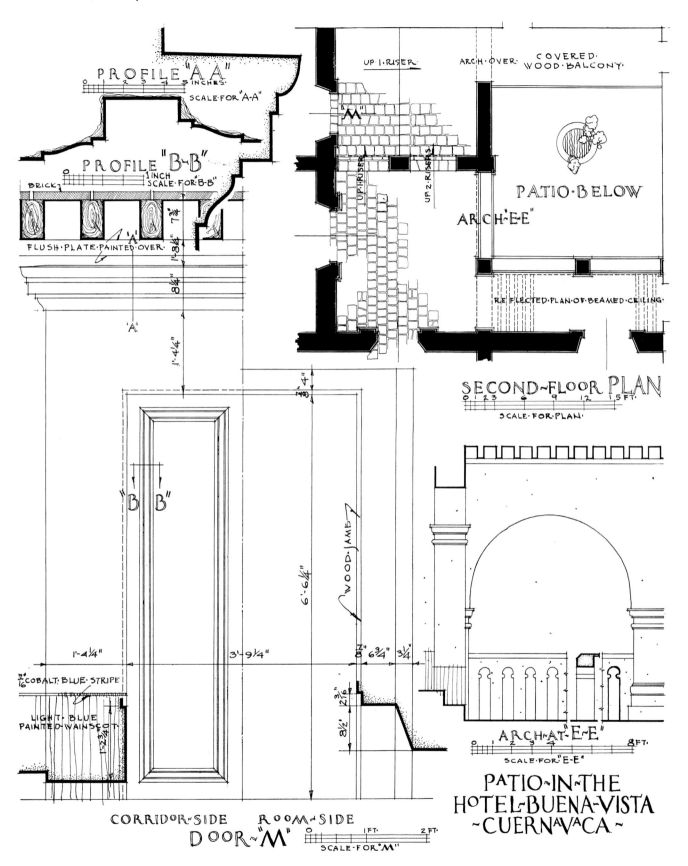

PROFILE "AA"
0 1 2 3 4 5 INCHES.
SCALE·FOR·"A·A"

PROFILE "B·B"
0 1 INCH
SCALE·FOR·B·B"

BRICK

FLUSH·PLATE·PAINTED·OVER·

UP·1·RISER

ARCH·OVER·

COVERED·
WOOD·BALCONY·

PATIO·BELOW

ARCH·E·E'

REFLECTED·PLAN·OF·BEAMED·CEILING·

SECOND~FLOOR PLAN
0 1 2 3   6   9   12   15 FT.
SCALE·FOR·PLAN·

"B·B"

WOOD·JAMB

COBALT·BLUE·STRIPE

LIGHT·BLUE·
PAINTED·WAINSCOT

1'-4¼"   3'-9¼"   6¾" 3¼"

ARCH·AT·E·E"
0 1 2 3 4   8 FT.
SCALE·FOR·"E·E"

CORRIDOR~SIDE   ROOM~SIDE
DOOR~"M"
0   1 FT.   2 FT.
SCALE·FOR·"M"

PATIO~IN~THE
HOTEL·BUENA·VISTA
~CUERNAVACA~

The Doctor's House. View of the garden facade. A brick paved terrace forms a level spot for garden furniture. The circle of masonry, called an arriate, which surrounds the tree on the right has a trough for water to protect against insects

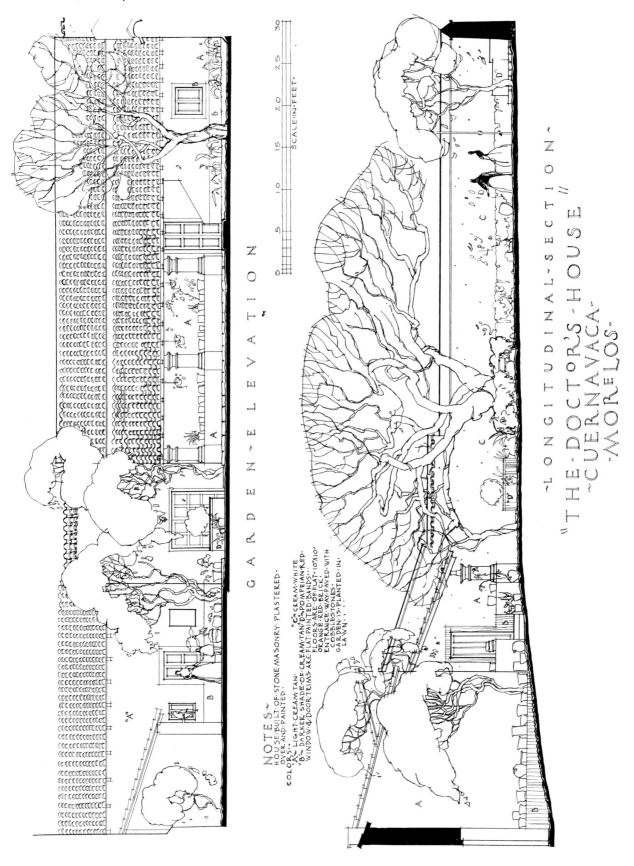

GARDEN·ELEVATION·

NOTES~
HOUSE·BUILT·OF·STONE·MASONRY·PLASTERED·
OVER·AND·PAINTED·
COLORS~
"A"~ LIGHT·CREAM·TAN· "C"~CREAM·WHITE
"B"~ DARKER·SHADE·OF·CREAM·TAN· "D"~POMPEIAN·RED·
WINDOW·&·DOOR·TRIMS·ARE·FLAT·PAINTED·BANDS···
FLOORS·ARE·OF·FLAT·10"X10"
ORANGE·RED·BRICK·
ENTRANCE·WAY·PAVED·WITH
COBBLE·STONES·
GARDEN·IS·PLANTED·IN·
LAWN···

·LONGITUDINAL·SECTION·
"THE·DOCTOR'S·HOUSE"
·CUERNAVACA·
·MORELOS·

SCALE·IN·FEET·
0   5   10   15   20   25   30

51

The Doctor's House. A view looking in from the entrance. The large spreading tree behind the fountain is a Cieba, a tree sacred to the Mayas

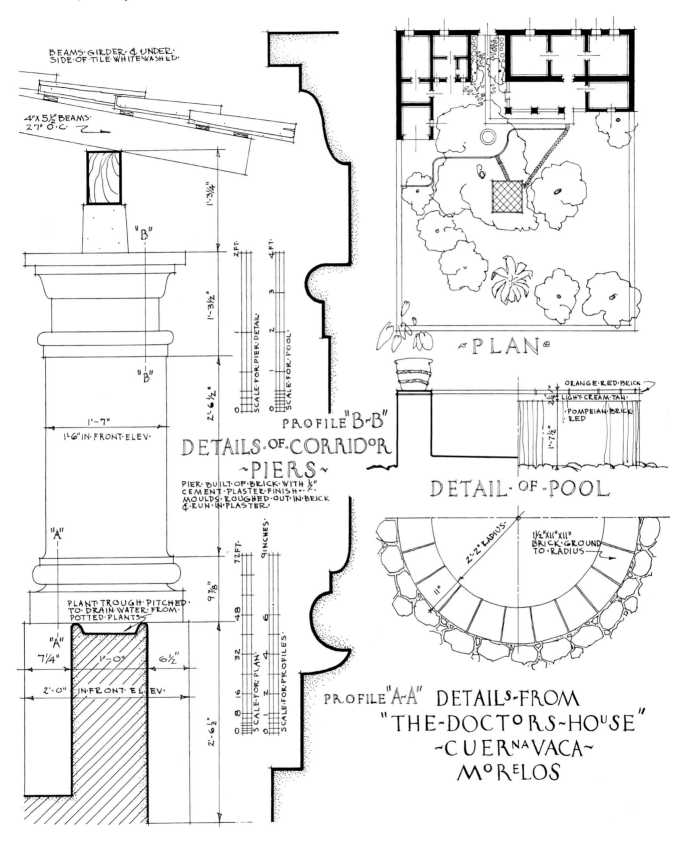

BEAMS·GIRDER·&·UNDER·
SIDE·OF·TILE·WHITE·WASHED·

4"·X·5½"·BEAMS·
27"·O·C·

1'-3¾"

1'-3½"

2'-6½"

"B"

"B"

1'-7"

1'-6"·IN·FRONT·ELEV·

2 FT.

3

4 FT.

SCALE·FOR·PIER·DETAIL·

SCALE·FOR·POOL·

PROFILE "B-B"
DETAILS·OF·CORRIDOR
~PIERS~

PIER·BUILT·OF·BRICK·WITH·½"·
CEMENT·PLASTER·FINISH··
MOULDS·ROUGHED·OUT·IN·BRICK·
&·RUN·IN·PLASTER·

"A"

9⅛"

PLANT·TROUGH·PITCHED·
TO·DRAIN·WATER·FROM·
POTTED·PLANTS·

"A"

7¼"

1'-0"

6½"

2'-0"·IN·FRONT·ELEV·

2'-6½"

72 FT.

48

32

8 16

SCALE·FOR·PLAN·

9 INCHES·

6

3

SCALE·FOR·PROFILES·

~PLAN~

ORANGE·RED·BRICK·

2¾"

LIGHT·CREAM·TAN·

POMPEIAN·BRICK·
RED

1'-7½"

DETAIL·OF·POOL

2'-2"·RADIUS·

1½"·XII"·XII·
BRICK·GROUND·
TO·RADIUS·

11"

PROFILE "A-A" DETAILS·FROM
"THE·DOCTORS~HOUSE"
~CUERNAVACA~
MORELOS

Above. A citarilla of shaped bricks. A citarilla is an open fence or balustrade usually built of shaped brick or tile. *Below.* View of the patio of an old tannery. Columns are built up of brick, plastered and painted

Patio of a casa de altos. A view toward the entrance. The open balustrade is of shaped bricks

Cuernavaca, State of Morelos

Patio side of a house. The arches, piers, and columns are of brick, plastered and painted a cream white. Door and window trims and dados are flat bands painted a pompeian red. The patio is cobble paved

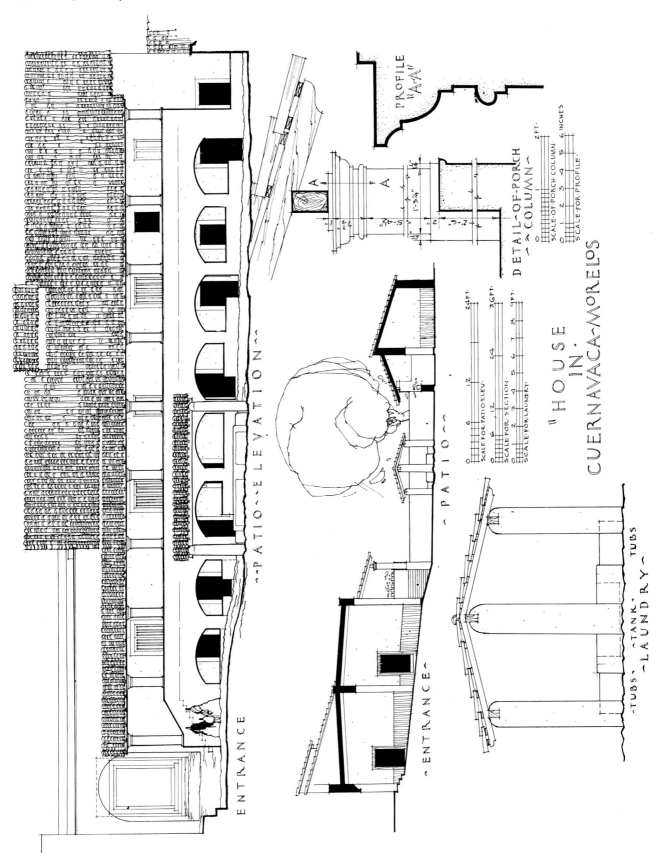

ENTRANCE

~PATIO~ELEVATION~

PROFILE "A·A"

DETAIL·OF·PORCH
~COLUMN~

~PATIO~

~ENTRANCE~

~TUBS~ ~TANK~ TUBS
~LAUNDRY~

"HOUSE
IN·
CUERNAVACA~MORELOS"

Two kitchen vents. Both built up of bricks. Except for the open brick louvres, they are plastered over and painted

Corner of the patio of a large two-story house. A masonry wall raises the planting above the pavement and protects it from insects. The moulds of the second floor balustrade are roughed out in brick, then run in plaster

View of Taxco from the Chapel of Oedo

BUILT in the shadow of great mountains which rise precipitously behind them, the hillside houses of Taxco look serenely down in turn on the crest and valley of many a lesser range. Torturous narrow streets weave a crazy pattern among the red tile roofs. The whole scene is picturesque in the extreme. Through four centuries this isolated place saw no wheeled vehicles. There are no sidewalks and the steep pitched roads are cobble paved from side to side. Nicely adjusted to unusual sites, the little houses are often planned on various levels. Some have their own walled yard or garden made possible by buttressed retaining walls of stone. The patio plan rarely occurs and the isolated house is not uncommon. Most of them are of adobe and, though well and strongly built, are distinguished by unusual lightness. They are painted various colors but always in soft shades. Wide-spaced rafters carry the roofs well beyond the walls and because of the frailness of these supports the weight of the tile must often be carried by wooden braces to the wall. Floors are paved with brick, ceilings frequently formed by light boards over wide-spaced beams. Tile in short lengths are used to build the graceful citarillos which inclose the terraced gardens and rail the open corridors.

Street facade of a dwelling. The entrance doorway is to an open yard from which one passes directly to various rooms of the house and to the open loggia above the street. A small shop occupies the far corner on the floor below

View of a dwelling from the rear. The street and entrance are on the level of the top break of the near wall. The columns of the porch pitch in slightly toward the house. The plastered adobe walls, much stained and weathered were originally painted a rich cream color

House of the Papaya Tree. The top floor front is the living room. A shop and storage rooms occupy the ground floor. Trims of doors and windows are flat painted bands

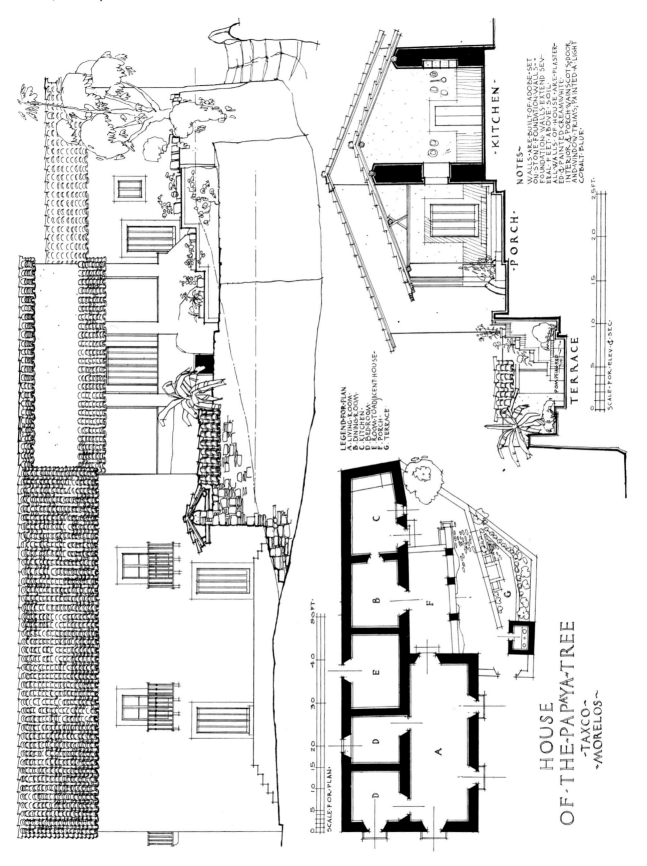

NOTES~
WALLS·ARE·BUILT·OF·ADOBE·SET
ON·STONE·FOUNDATION·WALLS·-
FOUNDATION·WALLS·EXTEND·SEV-
ERAL·FEET·ABOVE·SOIL·
ALL·WALLS·OF·HOUSE·ARE·PLASTER-
ED·&·PAINTED·CREAM·WHITE·
INTERIOR·&·PORCH·WAINSCOTS·DOOR·
AND·WINDOW·TRIMS·PAINTED·A·LIGHT·
COBALT·BLUE·

·KITCHEN·

·PORCH·

TERRACE

0 5   10   15   20   2.5 FT.
SCALE·FOR·ELEV·&·SEC·

LEGEND·FOR·PLAN
A·LIVING·ROOM·
B·DINING·ROOM·
C·KITCHEN·
D·BEDROOM·
E·ROOM·TO·ADJACENT·HOUSE·
F·PORCH·
G·TERRACE·

C

B   F

E   G

D

D   A

0 5 10 15 20 30   40   50 FT.
SCALE·FOR·PLAN·

HOUSE
OF·THE·PAPAYA·TREE
~TAXCO·
~MORELOS~

House of the Papaya Tree. *Above*. Hooded entrance gate. *Below*. Detail of the tile over the entrance gate. On the roofs beyond, pan and cover tile form the outside drip, paving tile the inside drip of the gable ends

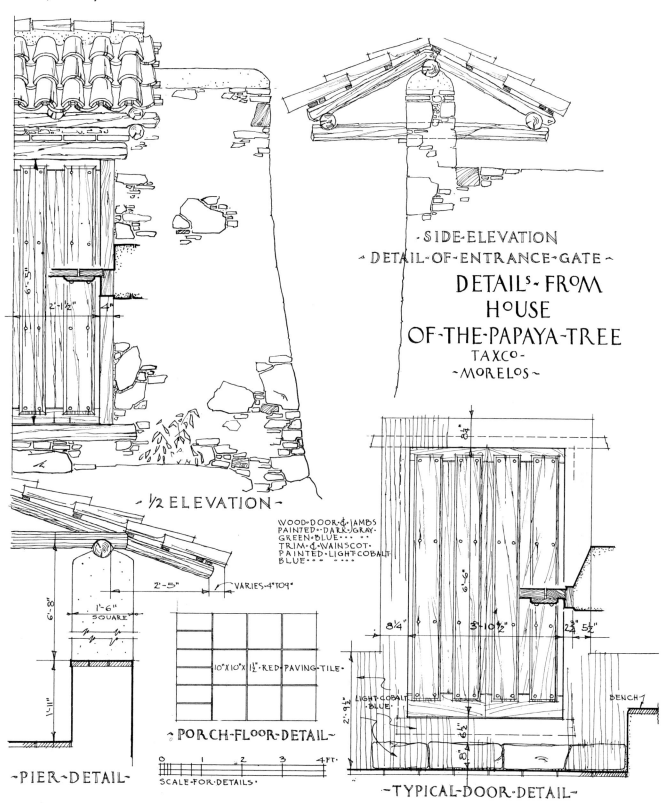

· SIDE · ELEVATION ·
~ DETAIL · OF · ENTRANCE · GATE ~

DETAILs · FROM
HOUSE
OF · THE · PAPAYA · TREE
TAXCO ·
~ MORELOS ~

~ ½ ELEVATION ~

WOOD · DOOR · & · JAMBS
PAINTED · DARK · GRAY
GREEN · BLUE · · ·
TRIM · & · WAINSCOT ·
PAINTED · LIGHT · COBALT ·
BLUE · · · · · · ·

VARIES · 4" TO 9"

2'-5"

1'-6"
SQUARE

6'-8"

1'-11"

10" X 10" X 1½" RED · PAVING · TILE ·

~ PORCH · FLOOR · DETAIL ~

0   1   2   3   4 FT.
SCALE · FOR · DETAILS ·

~ PIER · DETAIL ~

8¼"

6'-6"

8¼"   3'-10½"   2¾" 5½"

LIGHT · COBALT ·
BLUE ·

2'-9½"

6½"

8"

BENCH

~ TYPICAL · DOOR · DETAIL ~

House of the Bees. Patio side of the open corridor looking toward the entrance from the street. Spaces between the eave tiles are plugged full of chips of broken tile and mortar

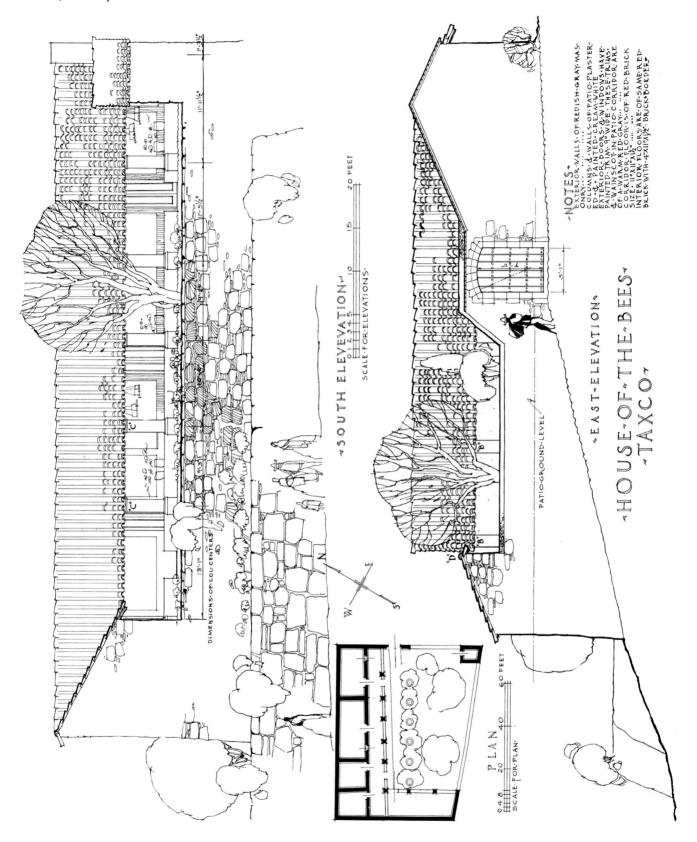

·SOUTH·ELEVATION·

SCALE·FOR·ELEVATIONS·

DIMENSIONS·OF·COL·CENTERS·

·EAST·ELEVATION·

PATIO·GROUND·LEVEL·

·HOUSE·OF·THE·BEES·
·TAXCO·

·NOTES·
EXTERIOR·WALLS·OF·REDISH·GRAY·MAS-
ONRY.···········
COLUMNS·&·WALLS·OF·PATIO·PLASTER-
ED·&·PAINTED·CREAM·WHITE.·············
EXTERIOR·DOORS·&·WINDOWS·HAVE·
PAINTED·TRIM·9"·WIDE·THESE·TRIMS·
&·WAINSCOT·IN·PATIO·CORRIDOR·ARE·
OF·A·WARM·RED·GRAY.··········
CORRIDOR·FLOOR·IS·OF·RED·BRICK·
SIZE·11"X11"X1½"···········
INTERIOR·FLOORS·ARE·OF·SAME·RED·
BRICK·WITH·4"X11"X1½"·BRICK·BORDER•

PLAN

SCALE·FOR·PLAN·

69

House of the Bees. *Above.* Interior view of the corridor. Under side of roof is left exposed. Floor of paving tile ten inches square. *Below.* Detail of wall treatment showing paving tile coping over end wall and roof tile drip over entrance

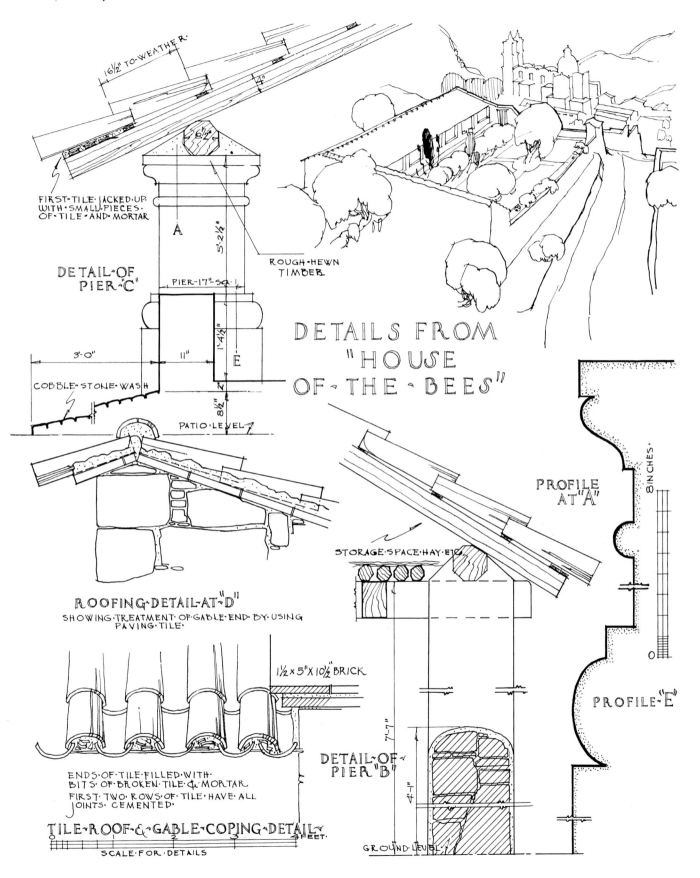

16½" TO·WEATHER·

FIRST·TILE·JACKED·UP·
WITH·SMALL·PIECES·
OF·TILE·AND·MORTAR·

ROUGH·HEWN·
TIMBER·

DETAIL·OF·
PIER·"C"

A

5'-2½"

PIER·17"·SQ·

1'-4½"

E

3'-0"

11"

2"

8½"

COBBLE·STONE·WASH·

PATIO·LEVEL·

DETAILS FROM
"HOUSE
OF·THE·BEES"

PROFILE
AT "A"

8 INCHES·

0

PROFILE·"E"

ROOFING·DETAIL·AT·"D"
SHOWING·TREATMENT·OF·GABLE·END·BY·USING
PAVING·TILE·

STORAGE·SPACE·HAY·ETC·

1½ x 5" X 10½" BRICK

DETAIL·OF·
PIER·"B"

7'-7"

4'-4"

ENDS·OF·TILE·FILLED·WITH·
BITS·OF·BROKEN·TILE·&·MORTAR·
FIRST·TWO·ROWS·OF·TILE·HAVE·ALL·
JOINTS·CEMENTED·

TILE·ROOF·&·GABLE·COPING·DETAIL·

0   1   2   3   4 FEET·
SCALE·FOR·DETAILS·

GROUND·LEVEL·

Two citarillos made of tiles about eight inches long. The one above is the railing of a porch overlooking the town. The one below is the top of a fence which separates the front yard of a house from the roadway

Interior view of a window. Wrought iron grille, solid wood shutters, head of wooden planks, plaster jambs, and paving tile sill. Walls are painted a cream white, dado a dark red

The Carpenter's House. View of the open corridor. The pathway is of earth and broken stone

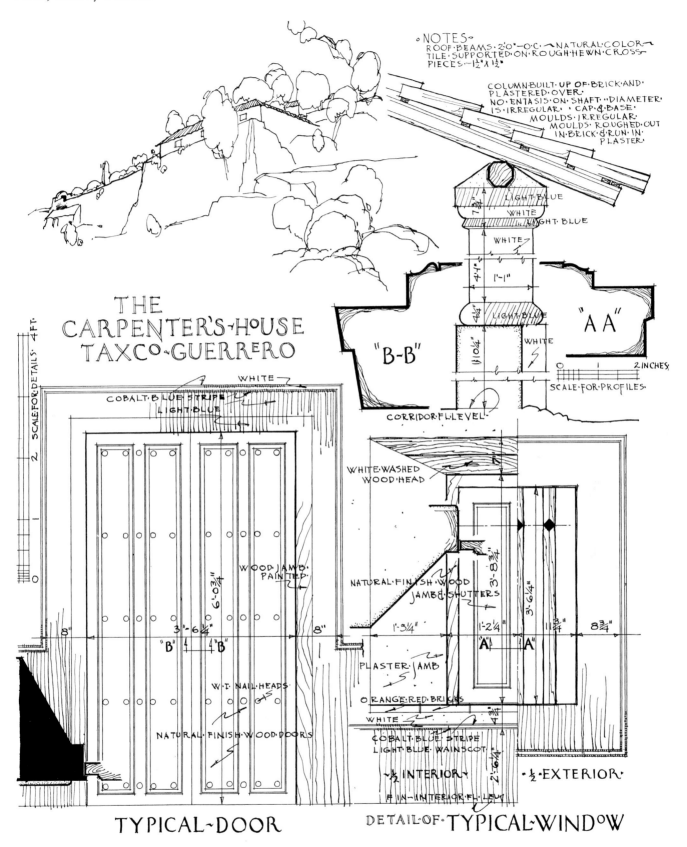

NOTES
ROOF·BEAMS·2'0"-O.C. · NATURAL·COLOR·
TILE·SUPPORTED·ON·ROUGH·HEWN·CROSS·
PIECES·1½"×1½"

COLUMN·BUILT·UP·OF·BRICK·AND·
PLASTERED·OVER·
NO·ENTASIS·ON·SHAFT· "DIAMETER·
IS·IRREGULAR· · CAP·&·BASE·
MOULDS·IRREGULAR·
MOULDS·ROUGHED·OUT·
IN·BRICK·&·RUN·IN·
PLASTER·

THE
CARPENTER'S·HOUSE
TAXCO~GUERRERO

LIGHT·BLUE
WHITE
LIGHT·BLUE
WHITE
1'-1"
LIGHT·BLUE
WHITE

"B-B"   "A A"

0   1   2 INCHES
SCALE·FOR·PROFILES.

CORRIDOR·FL·LEVEL·

SCALE·FOR·DETAILS·   4 FT.

WHITE
COBALT·BLUE·STRIPE
LIGHT·BLUE

WHITE·WASHED
WOOD·HEAD

6'-0¾"

WOOD·JAMB·
PAINTED·

NATURAL·FINISH·WOOD·
JAMB·&·SHUTTERS·

8"   3'-6¼"   8"

"B" | 4 "B"

1'-3¾"   1'-2¼"   3'-6¼"   1¾"   8¾"

"A" | "A"

PLASTER·JAMB·

W·I·NAIL·HEADS·

ORANGE·RED·BRICKS·

WHITE

NATURAL·FINISH·WOOD·DOORS·

COBALT·BLUE·STRIPE
LIGHT·BLUE·WAINSCOT·

·½ INTERIOR·   ·½ EXTERIOR·

FL·IN·INTERIOR·FL·LEV·

TYPICAL·DOOR   DETAIL·OF· TYPICAL·WINDOW

The Carpenter's House. Looking across the roof from above

The Carpenter's House. Interior view of the corridor

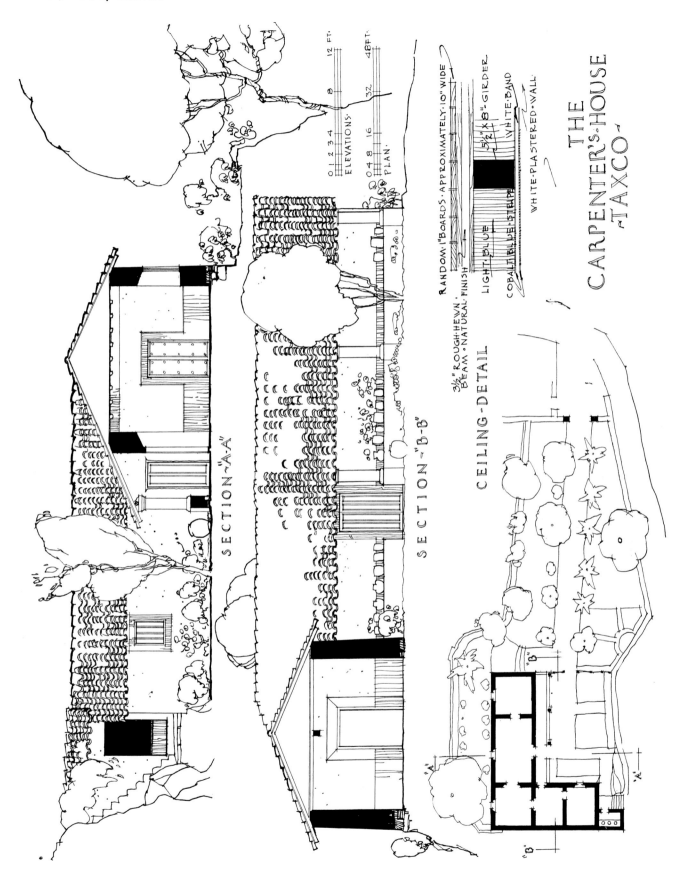

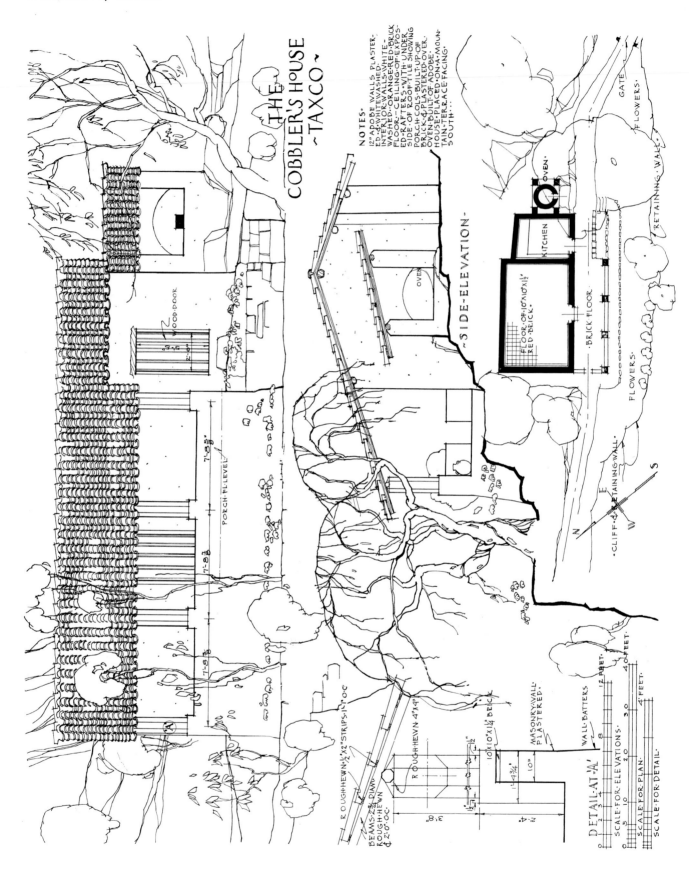

THE COBBLER'S HOUSE ~TAXCO~

· SIDE · ELEVATION ·

DETAIL · AT · 'A'

The Cobbler's House, built almost on the edge of a steep drop. The columns which lean in slightly make the little house seem more secure

The Butcher's House. The entrance is at the end of the porch to the right. Steps ramp down to a garden at the left

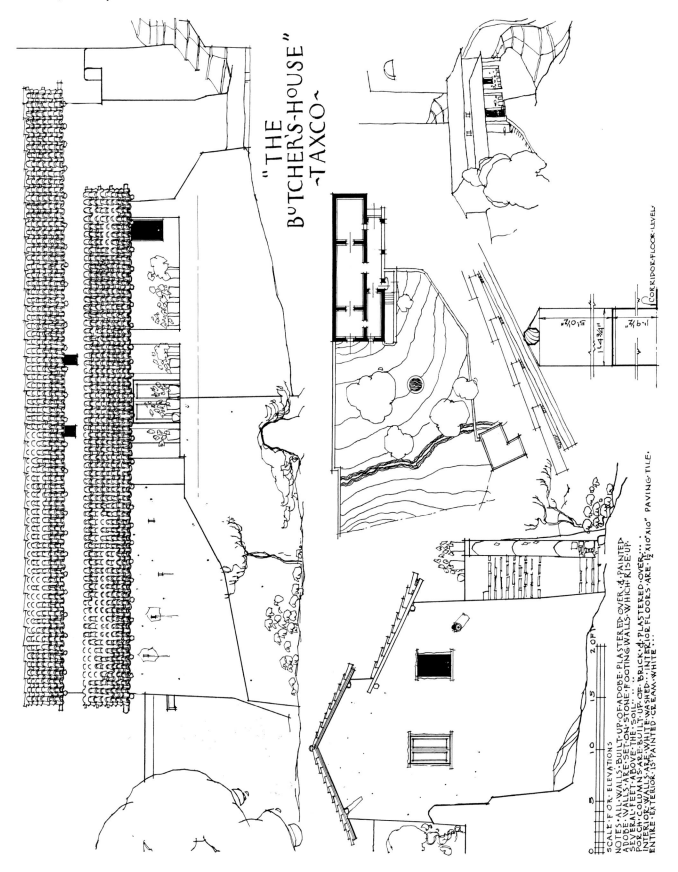

"THE
BⁿTCHER'S·HOUSE"
~TAXCO~

·SCALE·FOR·ELEVATIONS
·NOTES·ALL·WALLS·BUILT-UP·OF·ADOBE·PLASTERED·OVER·&·PAINTED·
·ADOBE·WALLS·ARE·SET·ON·STONE·FOOTING·WALLS·WHICH·RISE·UP·
·SEVERAL·FEET·ABOVE·THE·SOIL···...···
·PORCH·COLUMNS·ARE·BUILT·UP·OF·BRICK·&·PLASTERED·OVER···...···
·INTERIOR·WALLS·ARE·WHITE·WASHED···INTERIOR·FLOORS·ARE·12"x10"x10"·PAVING·TILE·
·ENTIRE·EXTERIOR·15"·PAINTED·CREAM·WHITE···...···

A view toward the plaza. The large roof shows the common practice of bedding the border tiles in mortar which is usually whitewashed

The Grocer's House. View of the facade. Door and window trims and the column caps are flat painted bands of cobalt blue. Walls are of adobe set on a masonry foundation several feet above the ground

The Grocer's House. The side wall of the living room. Decorated only with flat painted bands. The native chairs are green, with gold painted turnings, red knobs, canary yellow painted designs, and rush seats

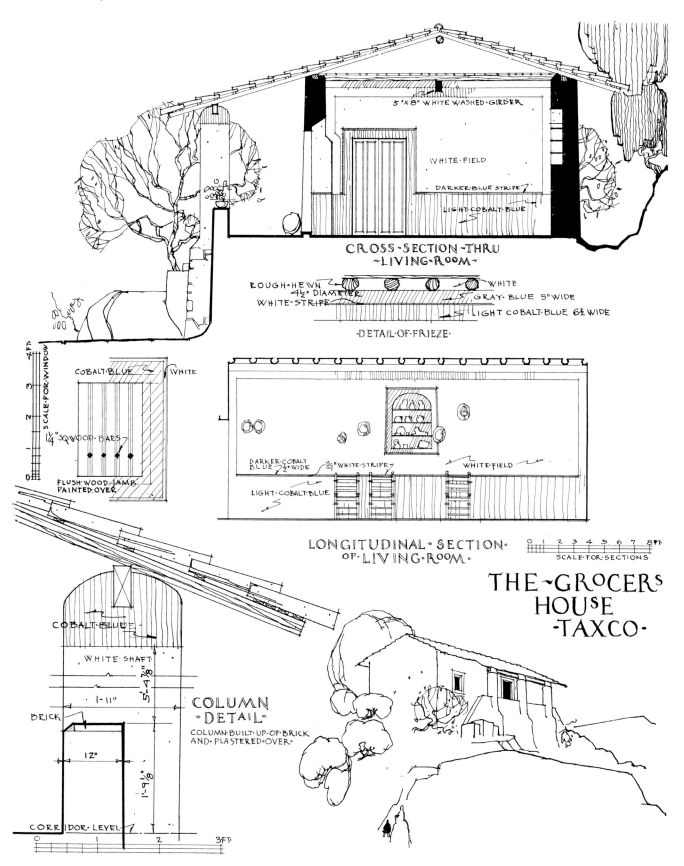

5"X 8" WHITE WASHED GIRDER

WHITE FIELD

DARKER BLUE STRIPE

LIGHT COBALT BLUE

CROSS SECTION THRU
~LIVING ROOM~

ROUGH HEWN
4½ DIAMETER
WHITE STRIPE

WHITE
GRAY BLUE 5" WIDE
LIGHT COBALT BLUE 6½ WIDE

DETAIL OF FRIEZE

SCALE FOR WINDOW 4 FT

COBALT BLUE   WHITE

1¼ SQ WOOD BARS

FLUSH WOOD JAMB
PAINTED OVER

DARKER COBALT
BLUE 7½ WIDE

¾" WHITE STRIPE

WHITE FIELD

LIGHT COBALT BLUE

LONGITUDINAL SECTION
OF LIVING ROOM

0 1 2 3 4 5 6 7 8 FT
SCALE FOR SECTIONS

THE GROCERS
HOUSE
TAXCO

COBALT BLUE

WHITE SHAFT

5'-4⅛"

1'-11"

BRICK

12"

1'-9⅛"

COLUMN
DETAIL

COLUMN BUILT UP OF BRICK
AND PLASTERED OVER

CORRIDOR LEVEL

0   1   2   3 FT

85

A citarillo of tile and brick combined above a retaining wall

A fringed gable end and fan-turned corner of tile

Taxco, State of Guerrero

Rear facade of a dwelling. The street on the opposite side is at the level of the upper floor. The braced extension of the roof to shelter the porch is not uncommon. The walls are of adobe, the buttresses of stone

A street in the village of Jacona. Walls are painted various shades of cream white, soft blue, yellow ochre, and greyed pink

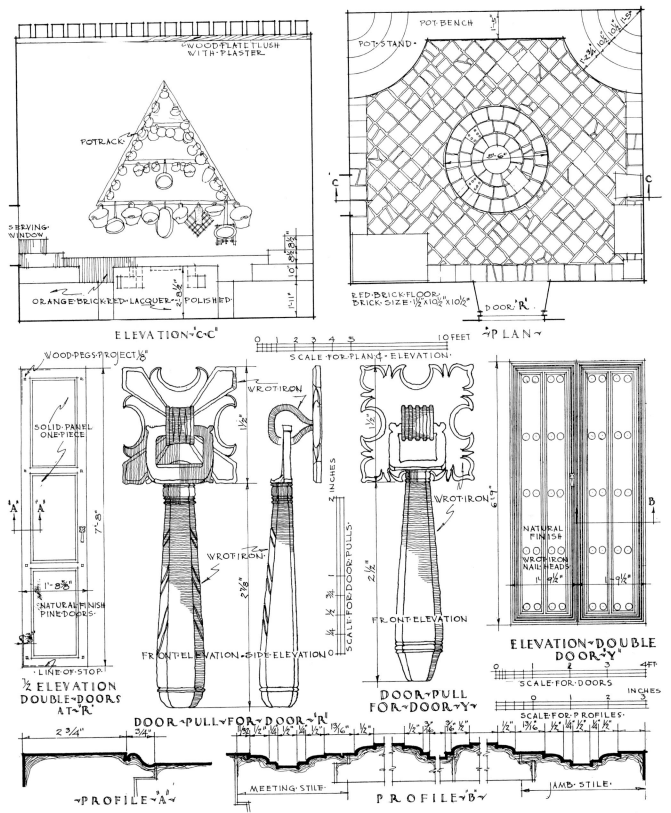

WOOD·PLATE·FLUSH·
WITH·PLASTER·

POTRACK·

SERVING·
WINDOW·

ORANGE·BRICK·RED·LACQUER· POLISHED·

8½"
10"
8½"
2·8½"
1'-11"

ELEVATION·"C·C"

POT·BENCH·
POT·STAND·
1'-5"
1'-2¾" 10½" 10½" 1'-5"
5'-6"

C   C

RED·BRICK·FLOOR·
BRICK·SIZE·1½"x10½"x10½"

DOOR·"R"·

~PLAN~

0 1 2 3 4 5   10 FEET
SCALE·FOR·PLAN·&·ELEVATION·

WOOD·PEGS·PROJECT·⅛"

SOLID·PANEL·
ONE·PIECE·

"A"   "A"

1'-8⅜"
7'-8"

NATURAL·FINISH·
PINE·DOORS·

·LINE·OF·STOP·

½ ELEVATION
DOUBLE·DOORS
AT~"R"

2¾"

WROT·IRON·
1½"

WROT·IRON·

2⅞"

FRONT·ELEVATION· ·SIDE·ELEVATION·

DOOR·PULL·FOR·DOOR·"R"

3 INCHES
¼ ½ ¾ 1
SCALE·FOR·DOOR·PULLS·

WROT·IRON·
1½"
2½"

FRONT·ELEVATION·

DOOR~PULL·
FOR~DOOR~"Y"

NATURAL·
FINISH·

WROT·IRON·
NAIL·HEADS·

1'· 9½"   1'· 9½"

6'·9"

B

ELEVATION~DOUBLE·
DOOR~"Y"

0   2   3   4 FT·
SCALE·FOR·DOORS

0   1   2   INCHES
0   1   2   3
SCALE·FOR·PROFILES·

¾"   1¾" ½" ¼" ½" ¼" ½" 13⁄16" ½"   ½" 3⁄16" ¾" ½"   ½" 13⁄16" ½" ¼" ½" ¼" ½"

MEETING·STILE·   JAMB·STILE·

~PROFILE~"A"~   PROFILE~"B"~

DETAILS·OF·A·KITCHEN ~~~ FROM·SALVATIERRA

The kitchen of a house in Salvatierra. Cooking is done on the large round brasero. Pots are placed on iron grilles over open charcoal fires. The holes on the sides make cleaning easy and allow a draft. Drawings are on the preceding page

Dining room of a house in Zamora. Walls are colored with water paint a cream white, the dado pompeian red. Furniture, except for the cupboard, is unfinished wood. Floor bricks are stained wine red

QUERETARO
1920
GEO. W. RUSTAY

The fountain of San Francisco

QUERÉTARO, a northerly town of the Aztec Empire, was captured by the Spanish in 1531. It is the center of a great agricultural and grazing district, and has been from earliest colonial days one of the provincial cities of first importance: wealthy, cultured, and proud of her important role in the romantic history of the Republic. This was the cradle of Mexican Independence, was the last refuge of the Emperor Maximilian. Although boasting many great houses of importance, the casas bajas of the seventeenth and eighteenth centuries best typify the Querétaran house. Generally they are of a fine grained limestone of the district, salmon pink in color. Each house fills its property to the sidewalk and is planned about one or more patios of moderate size. The zaguan entrances on the street rise almost to the ceiling, which may be as high as eighteen feet. Flat roofs are supported on heavy well-cut beams, spanned by long bricks, which are exposed on the inside to form the ceiling. Floors are paved with brick in various patterns, walls plastered and painted. Outside the windows are plainly trimmed with cut stone, there is a simple cornice of moulded members and there may be an exposed stone base. What sculpture or embellishment the house affords glorifies the entrance doorway.

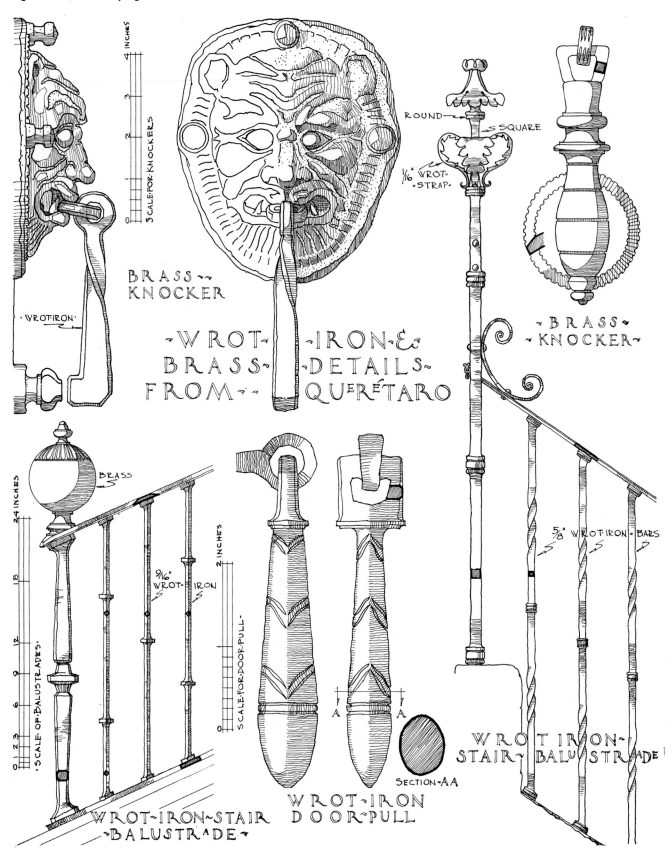

BRASS ~
KNOCKER

~VROT·IRON·

·VROT·IRON· &
·BRASS· ·DETAILS·
·FROM ~ ~ QUERÉTARO·

ROUND

SQUARE

1/16" WROT
·STRAP·

~BRASS~
~KNOCKER~

BRASS

24 INCHES

18

12

9/16"
WROT·IRON

6

·SCALE·OF·BALUSTRADES·

3
0 1 2 3

2 INCHES

·SCALE·FOR·DOOR·PULL·

4 inches

3

2

1

0

SCALE·FOR·KNOCKERS

A   A

SECTION·AA

5/8" WROT·IRON· BARS

WROT·IRON·
STAIR~ BALUSTRADE

WROT·IRON·STAIR·
~BALUSTRADE~

WROT·IRON
DOOR·PULL

94

House of the Blue Door. View of the patio. The custom of hanging potted plants on the walls is common throughout Mexico, especially among the poorer classes

House of the Blue Door. Walls are of masonry, plastered and painted. Stone trims are also painted

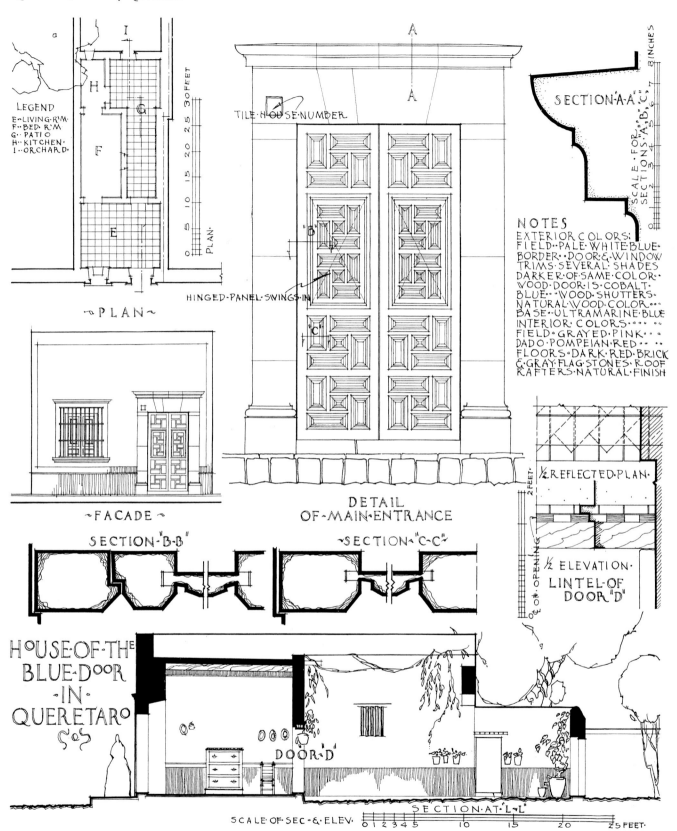

LEGEND
E·LIVING·R'M·
F··BED·R'M·
G··PATIO·
H··KITCHEN·
I··ORCHARD·

~PLAN~

TILE·HOUSE·NUMBER

SECTION "A·A"

SCALE·FOR·SECTIONS·"A","B","C"

NOTES
EXTERIOR·COLORS:
FIELD·PALE·WHITE·BLUE·
BORDER·DOOR·&·WINDOW·
TRIMS·SEVERAL·SHADES·
DARKER·OF·SAME·COLOR·
WOOD·DOOR·IS·COBALT·
BLUE·· WOOD·SHUTTERS·
NATURAL·WOOD·COLOR···
BASE·ULTRAMARINE·BLUE·
INTERIOR·COLORS··········
FIELD·GRAYED·PINK···
DADO·POMPEIAN·RED···
FLOORS·DARK·RED·BRICK·
&·GRAY·FLAG·STONES·ROOF·
RAFTERS·NATURAL·FINISH·

HINGED·PANEL·SWINGS·IN

~FACADE~

DETAIL
OF·MAIN·ENTRANCE

SECTION·"B-B"

~SECTION·"C-C"~

½·REFLECTED·PLAN·

½·ELEVATION·
LINTEL·OF·
DOOR·"D"

HOUSE·OF·THE
BLUE·DOOR
·IN·
QUERETARO

DOOR·"D"

SECTION·AT·"L~L"

SCALE·OF·SEC·&·ELEV· 0 1 2 3 4 5   10   15   20   25 FEET·

The House of Augustin Gonzales, an important residence of the late seventeenth century. The view is of the main patio from the entry. Steps and shallow ramps allow the stone paving to conform to the natural grade. Projecting stone canales drain the water from the flat tile paved roofs into the patio

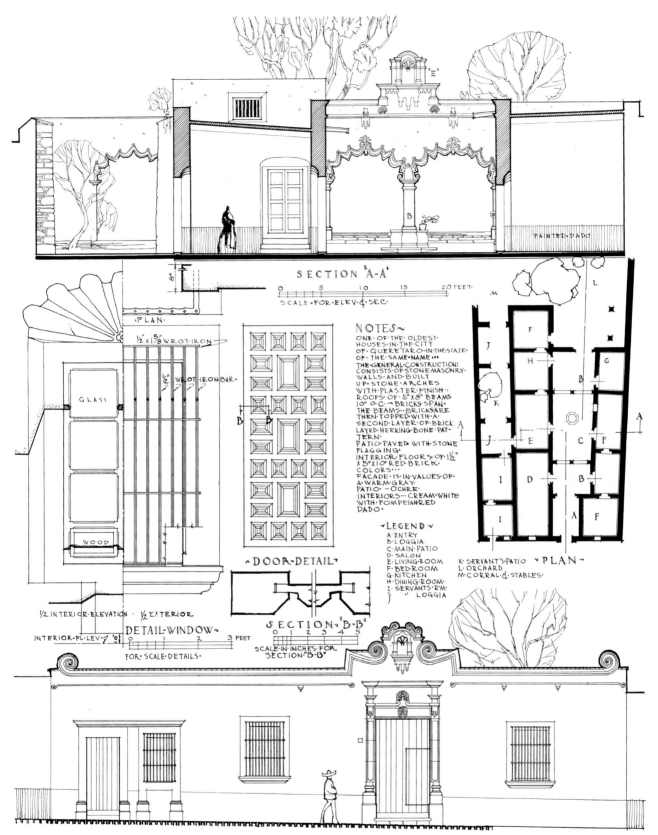

SECTION "A-A"

0   5   10   15   20 FEET
SCALE·FOR·ELEV·&·SEC·

·PLAN·

½ × 5/8 WROT·IRON·

½ WROT·IRON·BAR·

GLASS

WOOD

½ INTERIOR·ELEVATION · ½ EXTERIOR

INTERIOR·FL·LEV·

DETAIL·WINDOW~

0   1   2   3 FEET
FOR·SCALE·DETAILS·

·DOOR·DETAIL·

·SECTION "B·B"

0 1 2 3 4 5
SCALE·IN·INCHES·FOR·
SECTION "B·B"

·NOTES~

ONE·OF·THE·OLDEST·
HOUSES·IN·THE·CITY·
OF·QUERETARO·IN·THE·STATE·
OF·THE·SAME·NAME···
THE·GENERAL·CONSTRUCTION·
CONSISTS·OF·STONE·MASONRY·
WALLS·AND·BUILT·
UP·STONE·ARCHES·
WITH·PLASTER·FINISH·
ROOFS·OF·5"×8" BEAMS·
10"·O·C·~BRICKS·SPAN·
THE·BEAMS···BRICKS·ARE·
THEN·TOPPED·WITH·A·
SECOND·LAYER·OF·BRICK·
LAYED·HERRING·BONE·PAT-
TERN·
PATIO·PAVED·WITH·STONE·
FLAGGING·
INTERIOR·FLOORS·OF·1½
× 5"×10·RED·BRICK·
COLORS··
FACADE·IS·IN·VALUES·OF·
A·WARM·GRAY·
PATIO·─OCHRE·
INTERIORS─CREAM·WHITE·
WITH·POMPEIAN·RED·
DADO·

~LEGEND~

A·ENTRY·
B·LOGGIA·
C·MAIN·PATIO·
D·SALON·
E·LIVING·ROOM·
F·BEDROOM·
G·KITCHEN·
H·DINING·ROOM·
I·SERVANTS·R'M·
J·   "   LOGGIA·

K·SERVANT'S·PATIO·   ~PLAN~
L·ORCHARD·
M·CORRAL·&·STABLES·

PAINTED·DADO·

HOUSE·OF·AGUSTIN·GONZALEZ~QUERÉTARO

99

The House of Agustin Gonzales. The entrance doorway on the street

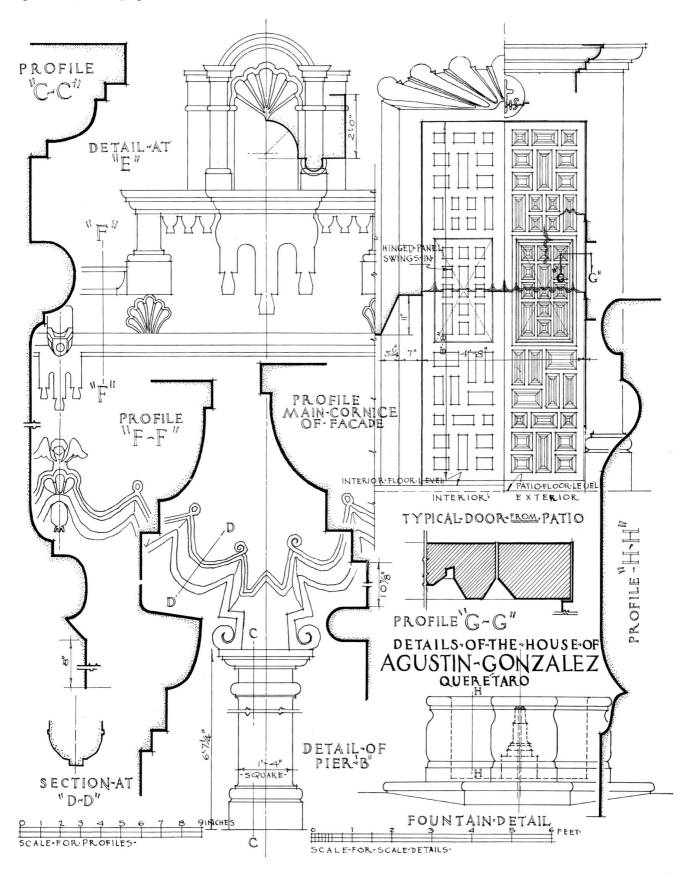

PROFILE "C-C"

DETAIL-AT "E"

"F"

2'-0"

HINGED-PANEL SWINGS-IN

"F"

"F"

PROFILE "F-F"

PROFILE MAIN-CORNICE OF-FACADE

11"

5¼" 7"

4'-8"

INTERIOR-FLOOR-LEVEL

PATIO-FLOOR-LEVEL

INTERIOR   EXTERIOR

PROFILE "H-H"

TYPICAL-DOOR-FROM-PATIO

D

D

10⅞"

PROFILE "G-G"

8"

6'-7¼"

DETAILS-OF-THE-HOUSE-OF
AGUSTIN-GONZALEZ
QUERÉTARO

C

H

SECTION-AT "D-D"

1'-4"
SQUARE

DETAIL-OF PIER-"B"

H

C

FOUNTAIN-DETAIL

0 1 2 3 4 5 6 7 8 9 INCHES
SCALE-FOR-PROFILES-

0   1   2   3   4   5   6 FEET-
SCALE-FOR-SCALE-DETAILS-

Above. Detail of a cornice of painted stone with a frieze of blue and white glazed tile. *Below.* A citarillo of shaped bricks, used to screen a rear yard from a small front patio

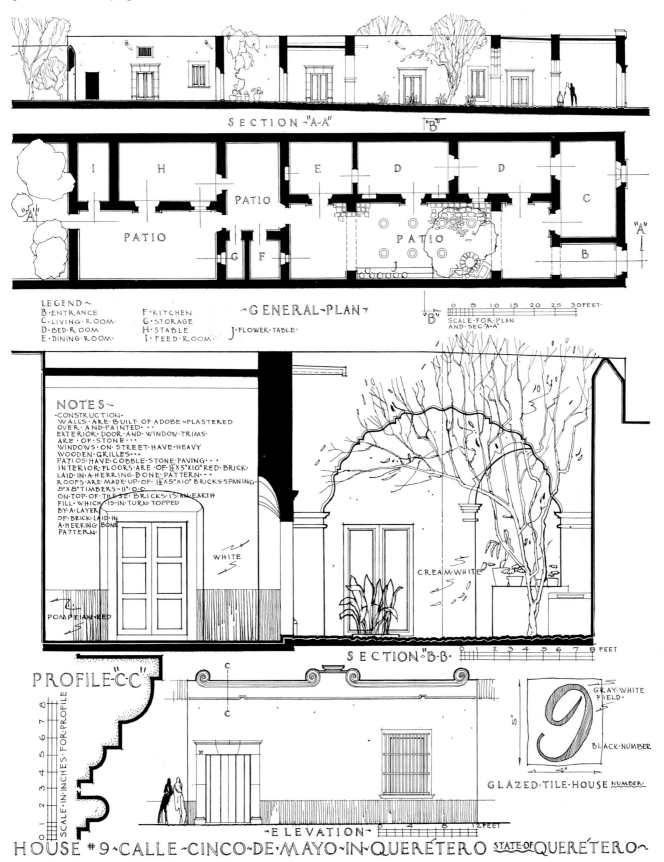

SECTION ·"A-A"· "B"

I H E D D

PATIO

PATIO PATIO C

"A" "A"

G F J B

LEGEND~
B·ENTRANCE   F·KITCHEN   ·GENERAL·PLAN·
C·LIVING·ROOM· G·STORAGE
D·BED·ROOM·   H·STABLE   "B"   0 5 10 15 20 25 30 FEET·
E·DINING·ROOM· I·FEED·ROOM· J·FLOWER·TABLE   SCALE·FOR·PLAN·
                                                    AND·SEC·"A-A"

NOTES~
·CONSTRUCTION·
WALLS·ARE·BUILT·OF·ADOBE~PLASTERED·
OVER·AND·PAINTED·
EXTERIOR·DOOR·AND·WINDOW·TRIMS·
ARE·OF·STONE···
WINDOWS·ON·STREET·HAVE·HEAVY·
WOODEN·GRILLES···
PATIOS·HAVE·COBBLE·STONE·PAVING·· ·
INTERIOR·FLOORS·ARE·OF·1½"X5"X10"·RED·BRICK·
LAID·IN·A·HERRING·BONE·PATTERN·· ·
ROOFS·ARE·MADE·UP·OF·1½"X5"X10"·BRICKS·SPANING·
5"X·8"·TIMBERS·11"·O·C·
ON·TOP·OF·THESE·BRICKS·IS·AN·EARTH·
FILL·WHICH·IS·IN·TURN·TOPPED·
BY·A·LAYER·
OF·BRICK·LAID·IN·
A·HERRING·BONE·
PATTERN·

WHITE

CREAM·WHITE

POMPEIAN·RED

SECTION·"B-B"·   0 1 2 3 4 5 6 7 8 FEET

PROFILE·"C-C"

SCALE·IN·INCHES·FOR·PROFILE 0 1 2 3 4 5 6 7 8

c
c

GRAY·WHITE·
FIELD·

5"

9

BLACK·NUMBER·

4"

GLAZED·TILE·HOUSE·NUMBER·

·ELEVATION·   0 4 8 12 FEET

HOUSE·#9·CALLE·CINCO·DE·MAYO·IN·QUERÉTERO· STATE·OF·QUERÉTERO~

House Number 9 on Calle Cinco de Mayo. A view of the main patio toward the entry. Drawings on plates 103 and 105

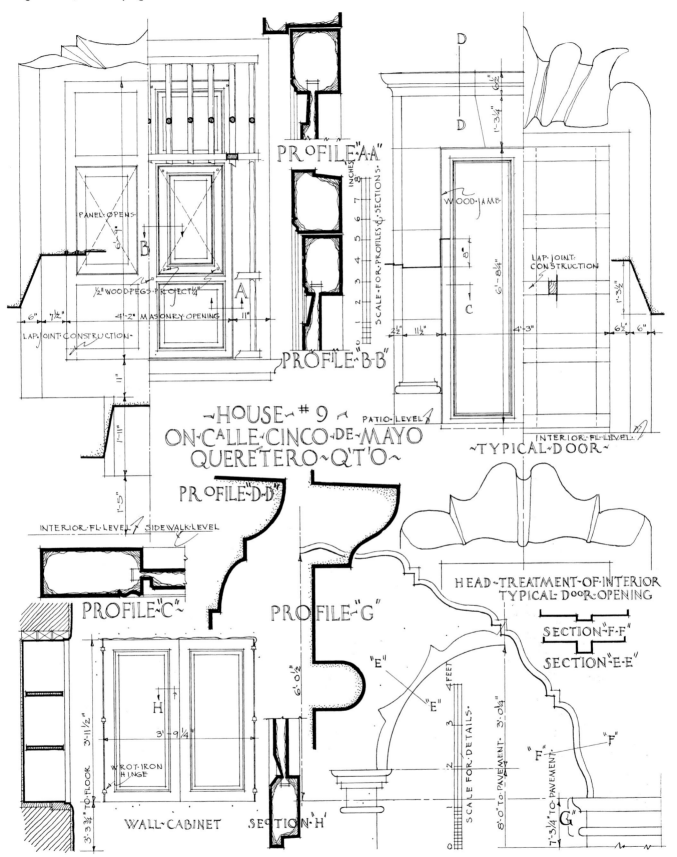

PROFILE "AA"

SCALE·FOR·PROFILES·&·SECTIONS·

INCHES

8 7 6 5 4 3 2 1 0

PROFILE "B-B"

PANEL·OPENS·

6'-9"

B

½"·WOOD·PEGS·PROJECT·¼"

A

6"   7½"   4'-2"·MASONRY·OPENING   11"

LAP·JOINT·CONSTRUCTION·

11"

1'-11"

1'-5"

D

D

6½"

1'-3¾"

WOOD·JAMB·

1'-8"

6'-8¼"

C

LAP·JOINT·CONSTRUCTION·

1'-3½"

2½"   11½"   4'-3"   6½"   6"

~TYPICAL·DOOR~

PATIO·LEVEL

INTERIOR·FL·LEVEL

~HOUSE~ #9 ~
ON·CALLE·CINCO·DE·MAYO
QUERETERO~Q'T'O~

PROFILE "D-D"

INTERIOR·FL·LEVEL   SIDEWALK·LEVEL

PROFILE "C"

PROFILE "G"

6'-0½"

HEAD·TREATMENT·OF·INTERIOR
TYPICAL·DOOR·OPENING

SECTION "F·F"

SECTION "E·E"

"E"

"E"

4 FEET

3

2

1

0

SCALE·FOR·DETAILS·

8'-0"·TO·PAVEMENT·   3'-0¼"

"F"

"F"

7'-3¾"·TO·PAVEMENT·

"G"

H

3'-11½"

3'-3¾"·TO·FLOOR

3'-9¼"

WROT·IRON·HINGE

WALL·CABINET

SECTION "H"

A corner of the patio of the Casa Faldon, a house of the early seventeenth century. Columns and arches are built of brick plastered and painted a deep greyed rose. The corridor is several steps above the stone paved patio

Meson de Santa Cruz. A view toward the entrance. A meson is a stopping place for both men and animals, principally the burro trains packing produce to town from the ranches

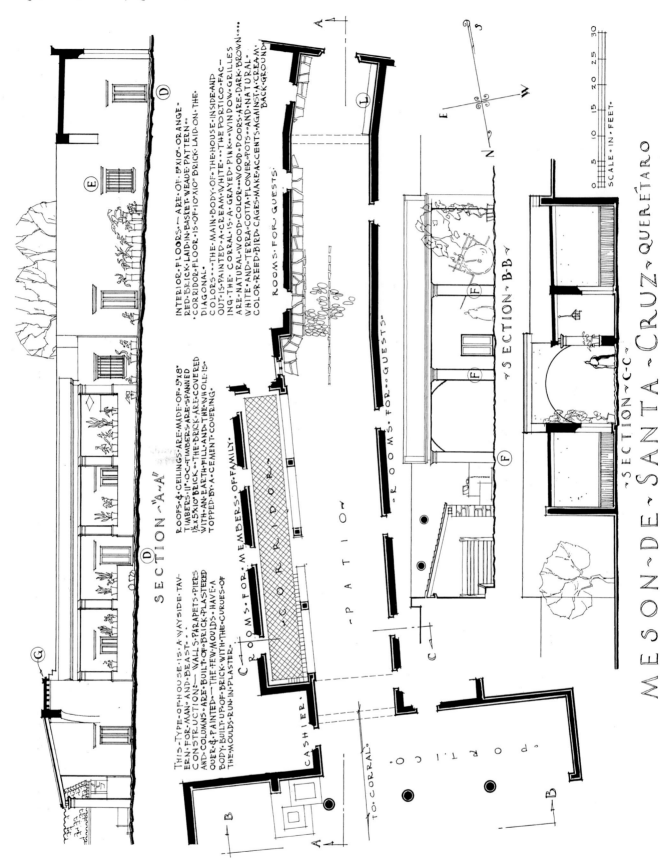

MESON DE SANTA CRUZ - QUERÉTARO

108

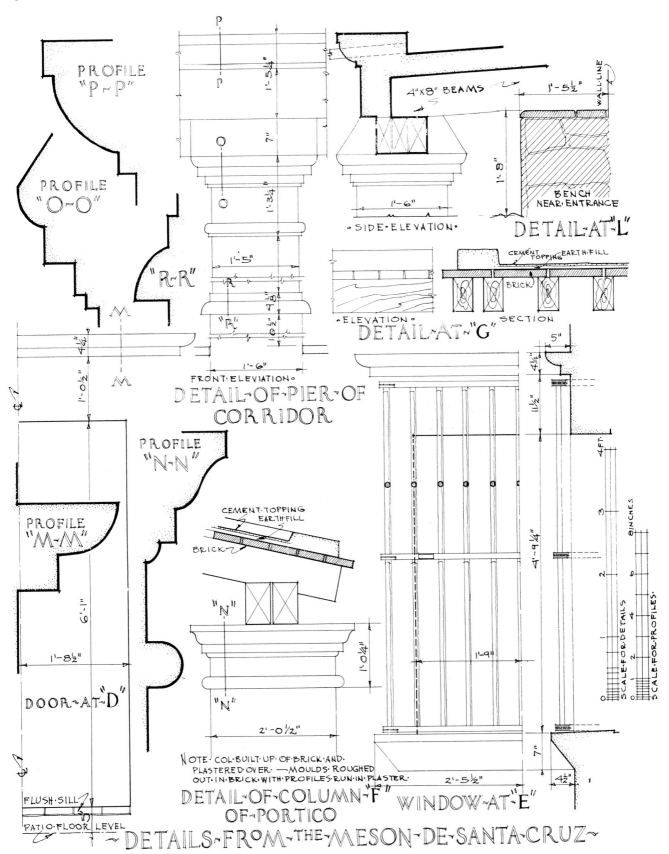

PROFILE "P~P"

PROFILE "O~O"

"R~R"

DETAIL·AT·"L"
BENCH NEAR·ENTRANCE

4"X8" BEAMS
1'-5½"
WALL·LINE
1'-8"

SIDE·ELEVATION
1'-6"

CEMENT TOPPING EARTH·FILL
BRICK
SECTION
ELEVATION
DETAIL·AT~"G"

FRONT·ELEVATION
DETAIL·OF·PIER·OF CORRIDOR
1'-5¾"
7"
1'-3¾"
1'-5"
4'8"
6½"
1'-6"

PROFILE "N·N"
PROFILE "M~M"

4¼"
1'-0½"

DOOR~AT·"D"
6'-1"
1'-8½"
FLUSH·SILL
PATIO·FLOOR·LEVEL

CEMENT·TOPPING EARTH·FILL
BRICK
"N"
"N"
1'-0¼"
2'-0½"

NOTE·COL·BUILT·UP·OF·BRICK·AND· PLASTERED·OVER.—MOULDS·ROUGHED OUT·IN·BRICK·WITH·PROFILES·RUN·IN·PLASTER.

DETAIL·OF·COLUMN~"F" OF·PORTICO

WINDOW~AT·"E"
5"
4½"
11½"
4'-9¼"
1'-9"
7"
4½"
2'-5½"

4·FT·
3
2
1
SCALE·FOR·DETAILS
8·INCHES
6
4
2
0
SCALE·FOR·PROFILES·

~DETAILS·FROM·THE·MESON·DE·SANTA·CRUZ~

Kitchen in the Casa de los Condes de La Cadena at Apaseo. The brasero formerly extended across the entire end. Part of the stone sink with shell back shows on the left

A Vecindad. Walls of masonry plastered and painted. From the top of the stair the bridge leads to rooms on the second floor rear

The Roofs of Patzcuaro

ROLLING wooded hills slope gently to a lake of unusual beauty. Along the shores and islands are numerous old towns and villages rich in the legend and tradition of an age-old past. The metropolis for all of these is the charming city of Patzcuaro which sprawls in a sunny hollow a mile beyond the lake. Tranquil, remote, of all the picture cities of Mexico this is perhaps the rinconcito, the little jewel of them all. Low tiled roofs are carried well beyond the walls to shelter the pedestrian against sun or rain. Mainly the houses are of adobe. Stone for building has been scarce while wood has always been abundant and much used for columns, balcony rails, and for the outside trim of doors and windows. Inside they use a painted dado and at times a painted frieze. The conchas over interior doors and windows are always very simple. Ceiling beams are often covered with thin boards instead of brick, sometimes with shakes laid herringbone between them.

A garden patio as seen from the entry way. The slender wooden columns and the horizontal window panes are typical of the houses of the district. Grass grows among the small stones that pave the open area

A small patio with corridor across the front side only. The columns and caps are of wood. Wood shakes across the projecting beam ends support a fill of brick and mortar below the tile. The frieze and dado are flat paint

The House of the Shields, a building with portales or covered walk, on the Plaza Grande. The columns, arches, window trims and shields are stone, the walls adobe, the narrow projecting bands connecting the windows are moulded bricks. The lower floor is occupied by shops

Above. Casa del Virrey. The very low first floor occupied by shops and quarters for servants and animals is typical of many Patzcuaran houses. The original turned wood balcony rail has been replaced by one of iron. *Below.* Facade of a house, painted light blue with trim and beam ends cream white and base dark red

Casa del Virrey. Two doors from an early seventeenth century house, the facade of which appears on the preceding page. On the right is a pair of doors on a front balcony with separate opening center panels. On the left is one of a pair painted grey blue

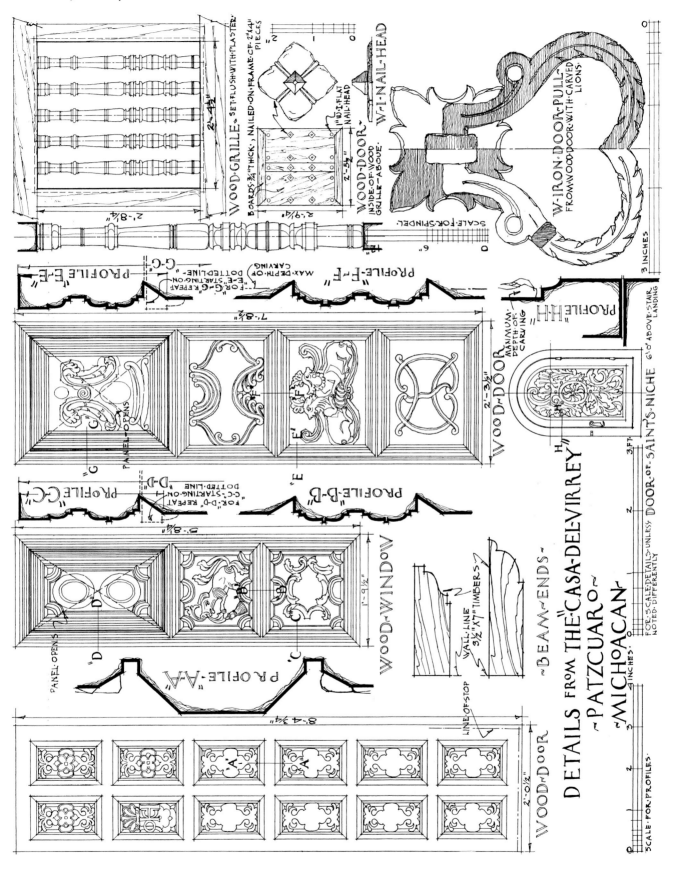

DETAILS FROM THE "CASA-DEL-VIRREY" ~PATZCUARO~ ~MICHOACAN~

119

Casa del Virrey. Carved wood door to a saint's niche on the stair

Casa del Virrey. A window with turned wood grille and wood door

Casa del Virrey. A pair of carved wood shutters on a window

Casa del Virrey. A pair of doors with panels of carved wood

Patzcuaro, State of Michoacan

Two kitchens typical of Patzcuaro. It is the custom for housewives to decorate the walls of their kitchens with an infinite variety of earthenware dishes and pots and pans, often using them to form interesting patterns on the walls

122

The kitchen of Doña Louisa Maria. Masonry shelves for the pots are topped with paving brick, the front is plastered, painted with red ochre, and polished to a lacquer finish as are the sides of the brasero, the corner of which shows in the foreground. Pots form the initials L. M. on the far wall

A view from the Plaza Grande looking toward La Compañia de Jesus. It is customary to use three principal colors on the facades, one for the dado, one for the walls, and another for the under side of the eaves

Patzcuaro, State of Michoacan

Calle de Quiroga. *Above.* A view looking toward the Plaza Grande. *Below.* A view looking up the street showing the entrance and facade of the Middle House and part of the entrance to the Lower House

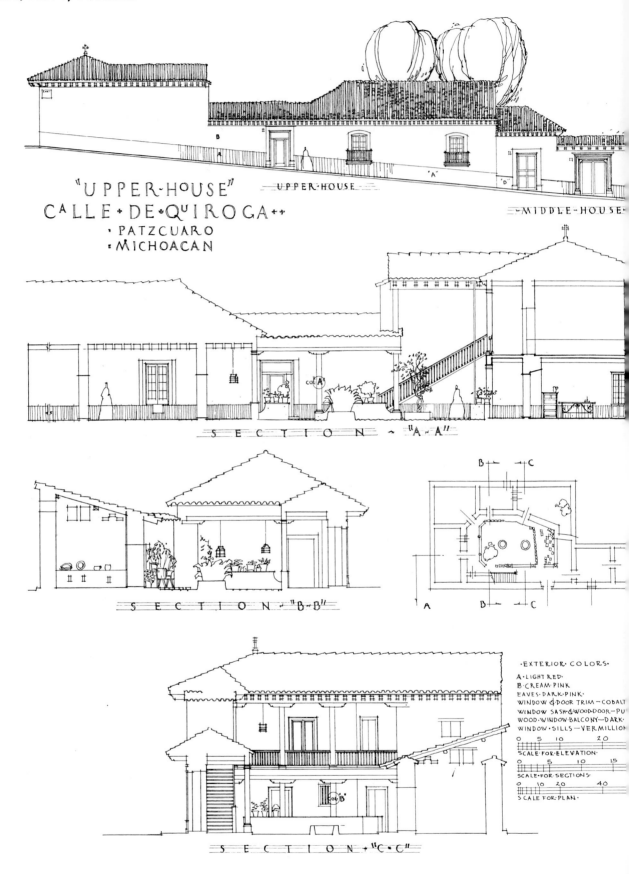

"UPPER·HOUSE"
CALLE·DE·QUIROGA··
·PATZCUARO
·MICHOACAN

UPPER·HOUSE

MIDDLE·HOUSE

SECTION ~ "A·A"

SECTION·"B·B"

SECTION·"C·C"

·EXTERIOR·COLORS·

A·LIGHT·RED·
B·CREAM·PINK·
EAVES·DARK·PINK·
WINDOW & DOOR TRIM—COBALT
WINDOW·SASH & WOOD·DOOR—PU
WOOD·WINDOW·BALCONY—DARK·
WINDOW·SILLS—VERMILLION

0   5   10   20
SCALE·FOR·ELEVATION·
0   5   10   15
SCALE·FOR·SECTIONS·
0   10   20   40
SCALE·FOR·PLAN·

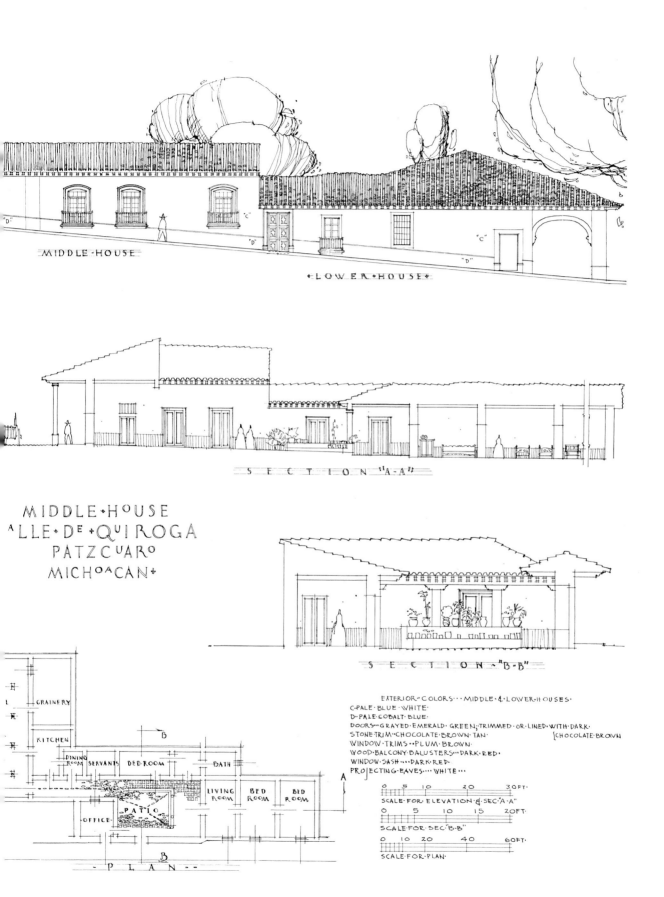

MIDDLE·HOUSE

·LOWER·HOUSE·

SECTION "A-A"

MIDDLE·HOUSE
ᴬLLE·Dᴱ·QᵁIROGA
PATZCᵁARᵒ
MICHᵒᴬCAN·

SECTION·"B·B"

GRAINERY

KITCHEN

DINING
ROOM   SERVANTS   BED·ROOM   BATH

OFFICE   PATIO   LIVING   BED   BED
                 ROOM   ROOM   ROOM

·PLAN··

EXTERIOR·COLORS···MIDDLE·&·LOWER·HOUSES·
C·PALE·BLUE·WHITE·
D·PALE·COBALT·BLUE·
DOORS···GRAYED·EMERALD·GREEN, TRIMMED·OR·LINED·WITH·DARK·
STONE·TRIM·CHOCOLATE·BROWN·TAN·   [CHOCOLATE·BROWN
WINDOW·TRIMS··PLUM·BROWN·
WOOD·BALCONY·BALUSTERS···DARK·RED·
WINDOW·SASH····DARK·RED·
PROJECTING·EAVES·····WHITE···

0   5   10   20   30 FT·
SCALE·FOR·ELEVATION·&·SEC·"A·A"

0   5   10   15   20 FT·
SCALE·FOR·SEC·"B·B"

0   10   20   40   60 FT·
SCALE·FOR·PLAN·

Calle de Quiroga. View of the patio of the upper house looking toward the high two-story side

Calle de Quiroga. The kitchen of the Middle House. Walls are painted cream pink, dado a dark red

Calle de Quiroga. Patio of the Upper House looking toward the low side. The valleys of the roof are made watertight by the use of a wood channel drain beneath the tile. Paving of small cobbles and flagging laid in an irregular checkerboard pattern

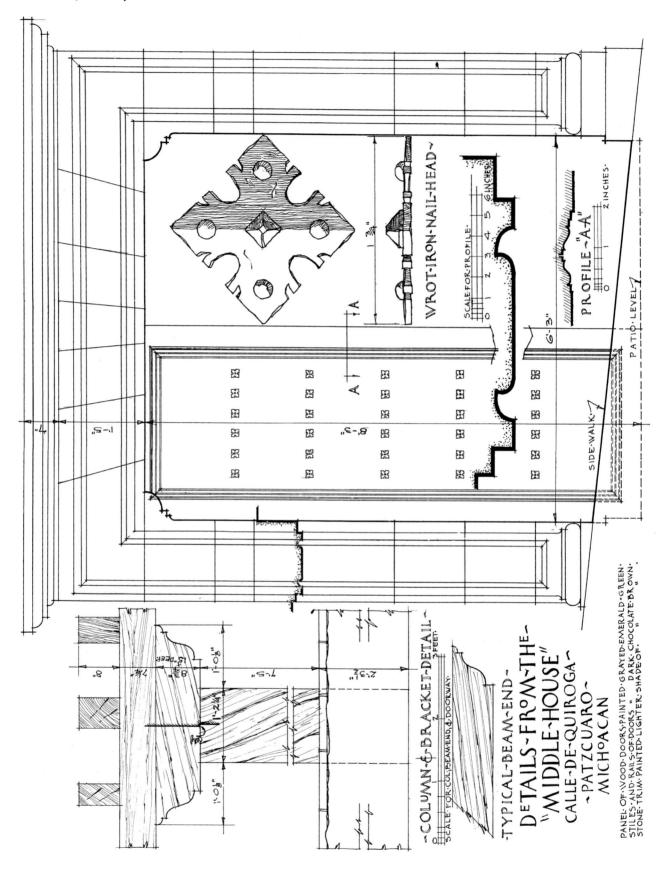

Patzcuaro, State of Michoacan

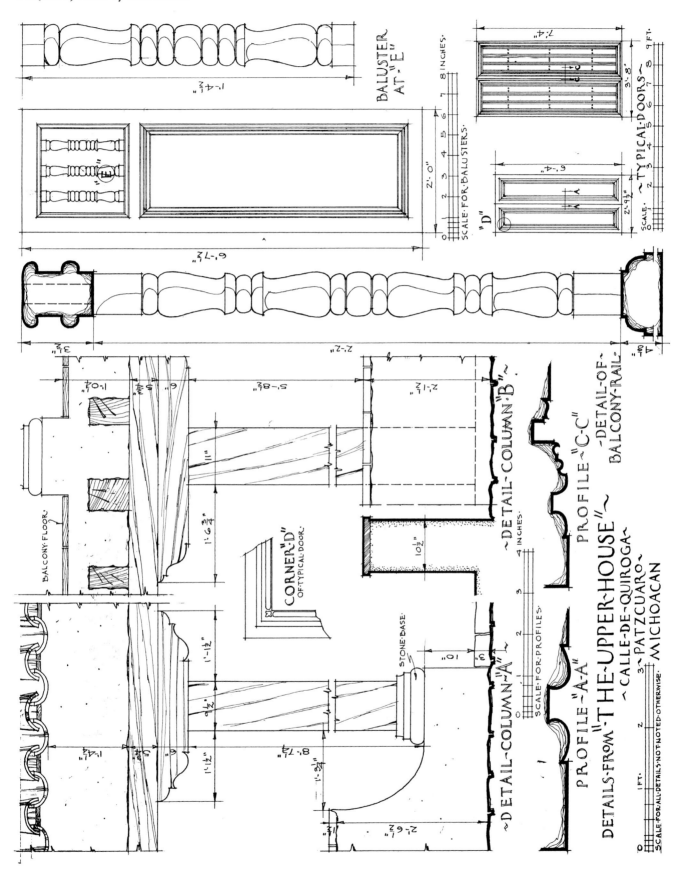

131

Calle de Quiroga. A view of the patio of the Middle House looking from the corridor toward the hooded entrance from the street

Calle de Quiroga. A view of the patio of the Lower House showing the exterior stairway and corridor protected by wide overhanging eves

Facade of a sixteenth century house on the Plaza Grande. Columns and girders are of wood, the walls of adobe plastered and whitewashed. Window sills are painted a brilliant vermillion. Shops and servants occupy the ground floor, the owner the floor above

GRAY

PAINTED·STONE
BASE·&·DOOR·
TRIMS·

TAN
RED·

WINDOW·TRIMS·ARE·GRAY·
SASH·ARE·YELLOW
BALUSTRADE·IS·BROWN·[MILLION
BALCONY·FLOOR·&·TOP·MOULD·VER·
PLASTERED·SURFACE·IS·
A·CREAM·COLOR·
BRACKETS·ARE·DARKER
CREAM·
FRIEZE·BOARD·IS·TAN·
WOOD·COL·BRACKETS·&·
GIRDER·ARE·DARK·GRAY·TAN

THIS·MUCH·FOR·"B-B"

"CC"·SAME·AS·"A-A"·BUT·
STARTS·ON·DOTTED·
LINE·

BUILT·UP·WOOD
GIRDER·

PROFILE·"A-A"·WITH·"B-B"·&·"C-C"   "D-D"

HOUSE
ON
THE·PLAZA,
·PATZCUARO·
MICHºACAN

0   1   2 INCHES 3
SCALE·FOR·PROFILES

0   1 FOOT
SCALE·FOR·COLUMN·

0   1   2   3 FT
SCALE·FOR·DOOR·

0 1 2 3 4   8   12 FT
SCALE·FOR·ELEV·&·SECTION·

HINGED·
PANEL·SWINGS·SEPARATELY

7'-2"

3'-5 3/8"

2 3/4"   11 1/2"

SIDEWALK·LEVEL

8"

INTERIOR·FL·LEVEL

A dipping fountain and tower which ventilates an underground aqueduct. Fountain and tower above the eaves are painted a greyed light red. The wall is cream white

Patzcuaro, State of Michoacan

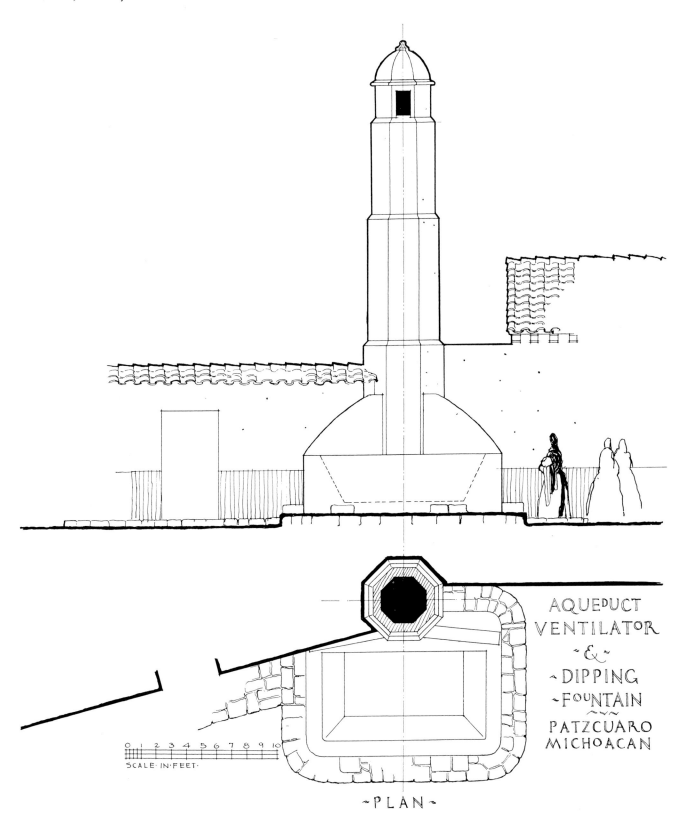

AQUEDUCT
VENTILATOR
~&~
~DIPPING
~FOUNTAIN
~~
PATZCUARO
MICHOACAN

0 1 2 3 4 5 6 7 8 9 10
·SCALE·IN·FEET·

~PLAN~

137

A typical street of Patzcuaro. The wide eaves which shelter the narrow sidewalks are formed by extending the ceiling beams beyond the walls. These in turn support the rafters. The trim around the windows of the third house is of wood

Porton of a small house. A porton screens the patio from the entry way, affording some protection while the great doors of the zaguan stand open during the day. It permits a view and allows a free circulation of air

Open corridor of the Hospital de Fray Juan de San Miguel, a sixteenth century building. Beams are unusually heavy and widely spaced

Two houses in Morelia. The piers, column, arches, and coping of the upper one are painted stone. The wall is painted plaster

A small house on the outskirts of San Miguel de Allende. It is of the type called casa poblana. The bench beside the door, the potted plants, and earthenware hung on the wall are the usual features of a modest house

Above. A typical flat roofed adobe house. The plaster is carried down to cover the rock face below. Base, window trim, and outside border band are red, inside border band a lighter red, and field a cream pink. *Below.* House at an orchard. A door is the only opening in the outside wall along the highway

Laundry trays in front of the public baths. They are painted dark red and polished to a lacquer finish. Clean water flows in a trough on one side, used water flows out in a trough on the opposite side

Cupboard doors in a dwelling. They are natural wood finish and about six feet high

LOS·REYES
1929
GEO·W·RUSTAY

The South Hill

THROUGH the deep-cleft Canyon de Marfil, a mountain road winds up to Guanajuato. Famous as a mining city, her fabulous shafts for centuries filled the coffers of the Spanish Crown, built private fortunes, and enriched the church. Facing each other across the narrow gorge, time-scarred adobe houses cling stubbornly along the crooked roads to where the bluffs rise barren and russet above a fringe of nopal cactus. The streets themselves are tiny canyons a few feet wide, their climb often broken by steep flights of steps. The floor of one house may be above the neighbor's roof. Entrance is often from stoops unusually high, windows are smaller, fewer, doors less featured than in most districts. Though void of any ornament, save the ever-present mesetas, the little painted houses with their broken planes and interesting masses are remarkably effective. The patio when used is carried high above the street on a terrace wall and opens to a prospect as striking and as picturesque as any in all Mexico.

The facade of a hillside house. Adobe walls are plastered and painted a light blue, trimmed with flat bands and dado of a darker blue. Flat roofs and copings are of paving tile. Rooms are on various levels

A view along the Calle de los Positas, formerly the most important street of the city

House on the South Hill. Walls are of adobe plastered and painted. Stone foundation walls are carried up to the patio level. A stone canal carries the water from the patio floor. Canales from the flat roofs are of terra cotta. The walls are free of all mouldings

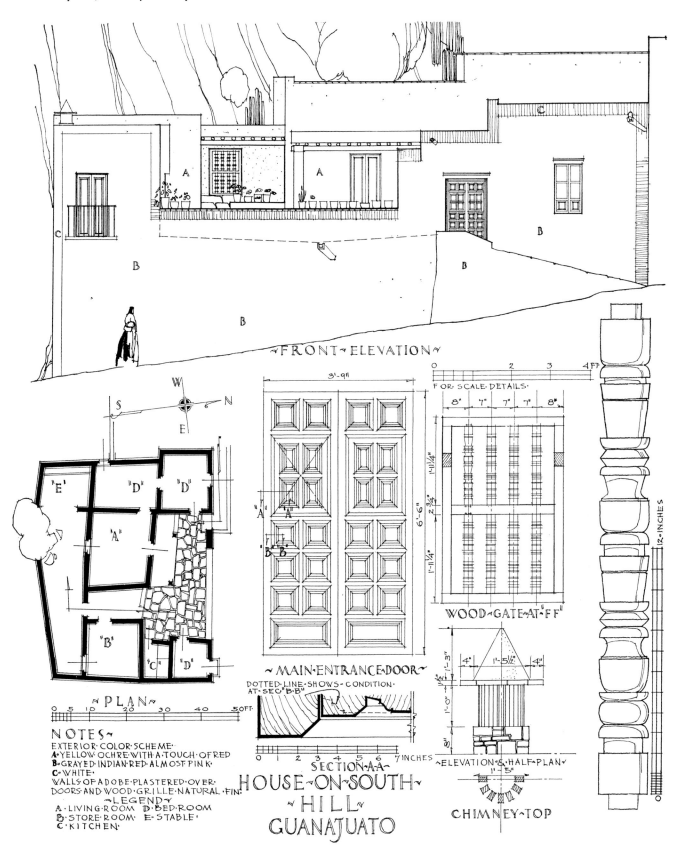

~FRONT~ELEVATION~

~PLAN~

0 5 10 20 30 40 50 FT.

NOTES~
EXTERIOR·COLOR·SCHEME·
A·YELLOW·OCHRE·WITH·A·TOUCH·OF·RED
B·GRAYED·INDIAN·RED·ALMOST·PINK·
C·WHITE·
WALLS·OF·ADOBE·PLASTERED·OVER·
DOORS·AND·WOOD·GRILLE·NATURAL·FIN:
~LEGEND~
A·LIVING·ROOM   D·BED·ROOM
B·STORE·ROOM   E·STABLE·
C·KITCHEN·

3'-9"

6'-6"

~MAIN·ENTRANCE·DOOR~
DOTTED·LINE·SHOWS·CONDITION·
AT·SEC·"B·B"

0 1 2 3 4 5 6 7 INCHES

~SECTION·A·A~

HOUSE~ON·SOUTH
~HILL~
GUANAJUATO

0   2   3   4 FT.
·FOR·SCALE·DETAILS·

8"   7"   7"   7"   8"

~WOOD~GATE·AT·"FF"

4"   1'-5½"   4"

~ELEVATION·&·HALF·PLAN~
1'-5"
CHIMNEY·TOP

12·INCHES

151

House on the North Hill. Walls are of adobe, plastered and water-painted. Copings are of paving tiles. Floor and brackets of the balcony are of thin stone slabs

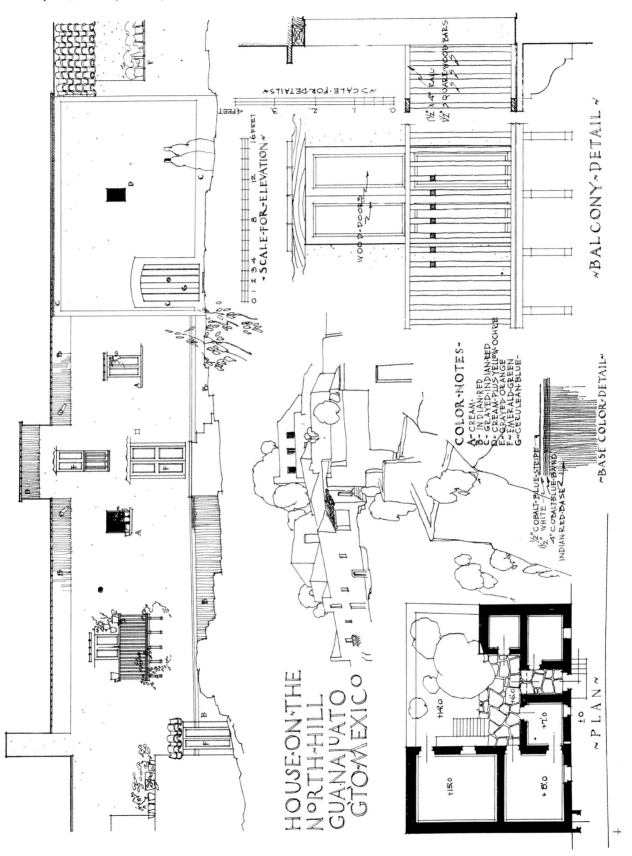

COLOR-NOTES-

A- CREAM.
B- INDIAN-RED
C- GRAYED-INDIAN-RED
D- CREAM-PLUS-YELLOW-OCHRE
E- GRAYED-ORANGE
F- EMERALD-GREEN
G- CERULEAN-BLUE-

1/2" COBALT-BLUE-STRIPE
1/2" WHITE
1/2" COBALT-BLUE-BAND
4" COBALT-BLUE-BAND
INDIAN-RED-BASE

~BASE COLOR-DETAIL~

~BALCONY-DETAIL~

1 1/2" X 4" RAIL
1/2" SQUARE-WOOD-BARS

WOOD-DOORS

~SCALE-FOR-DETAILS~
3 2 1 0

~SCALE-FOR-ELEVATION~
0 1 2 3 4   8   12   16 FEET
4 FEET

HOUSE-ON-THE
NORTH-HILL
GUANAJUATO
GTO-MEXICO

~PLAN~

+15.0
+8.0
+14.0
+6.0
+7.0
+0

House of the Conde Rul at Valenciana, near Guanajuato. View of the facade on the plaza. Walls are of masonry plastered and painted a greyed cream rose, which is almost the same color as the cut stone trim of door and windows

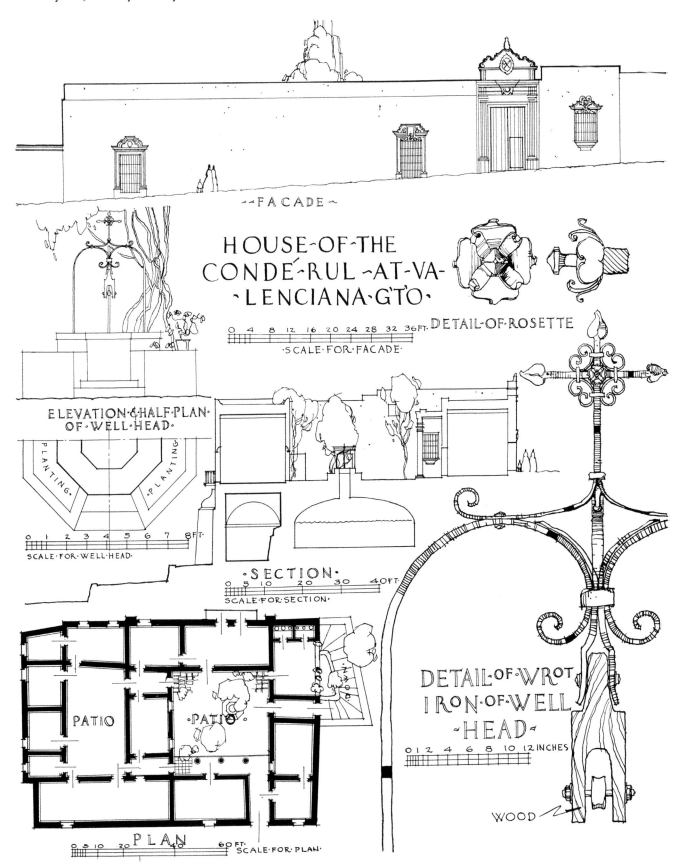

~FACADE~

HOUSE-OF-THE
CONDE-RUL -AT-VA-
-LENCIANA-GTO-

DETAIL-OF-ROSETTE

0 4 8 12 16 20 24 28 32 36FT.
·SCALE·FOR·FACADE·

ELEVATION·&·HALF·PLAN·
OF·WELL·HEAD·

PLANTING.   ·PLANTING·

0 1 2 3 4 5 6 7 8FT.
SCALE·FOR·WELL·HEAD.

·SECTION·
0 5 10 20 30 40FT.
SCALE·FOR·SECTION·

DETAIL·OF·WROT
IRON·OF·WELL
~HEAD~

0 1 2 4 6 8 10 12 INCHES

WOOD

PATIO   ·PATIO·

PLAN
0 5 10 20 40 60FT.   SCALE·FOR·PLAN·

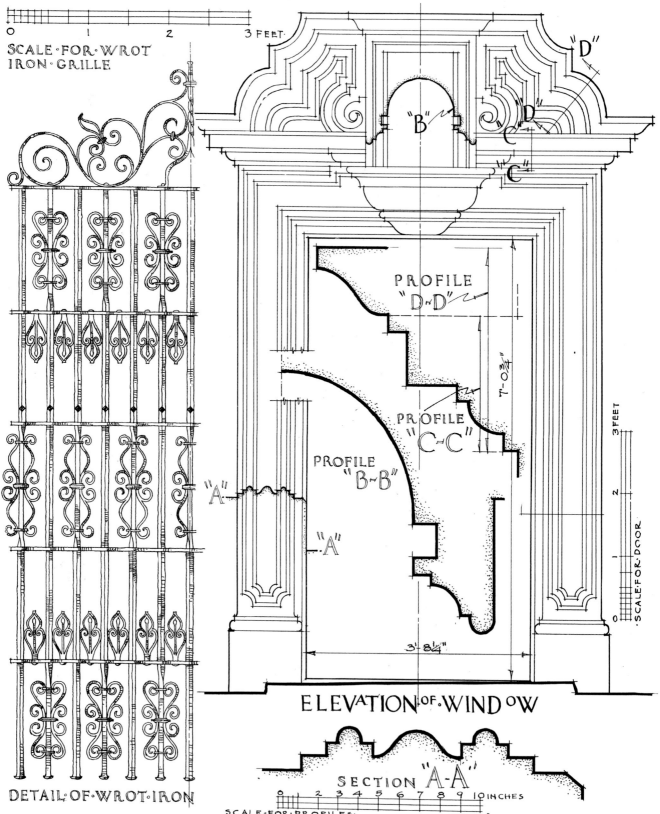

0   1   2   3 FEET
SCALE·FOR·WROT
IRON·GRILLE

DETAIL·OF·WROT·IRON

"A"

"A"

PROFILE
"B~B"

PROFILE
"C~C"

PROFILE
"D~D"

"D"

"B"

"C"
"C"

"D"

7'-0 3/4"

3'-8 1/4"

3 FEET

2

1

0

·SCALE·FOR·DOOR·

ELEVATION·OF·WINDOW

SECTION "A-A"

0   2   3   4   5   6   7   8   9   10 INCHES
·SCALE·FOR·PROFILES·

DETAILS·FROM·THE·HOUSE·OF·THE·CONDÉ·RUL·AT·VALENCIANA

House of the Conde Rul at Valenciana, near Guanajuato. Window with a wrought iron grille. A carved stone figure is missing from the niche above

House of the Conde Rul. Small window on right of the entrance

House of the Conde Rul. Entrance doorway looking into the patio

A window on the street facade of a house of the sixteenth century. Neither the solid wood shutters nor the wrought iron grille are original. The cut stone trim is painted cream white, the wall is a yellow ochre, and the base a dark red

COAYOCAN
1924
GEO W. RUSTAY.

Floor in the house of the Marquesa

THE house of the Marquesa de Uluapa is a house of the middle eighteenth century. Although it cannot properly be called representative, it does reflect the elegant and extravagant life of the period, to which it was no doubt ideally suited. Two centuries had passed since the days of the conquistadores, vast fortunes had accumulated, and the noble families lived in a manner comparable to their European cousins. Most of the private palaces were on a scale far grander than that of the Marquesa, though of no more than equal pretension, and there were few so much adorned, perhaps because the dueña of this house was a lady. The entrance from the street is directly opposite the stairway. On the walls are some famous examples of work in lozo. Glazed tiles of the usual size are placed together to form large panels, and done on them in various colors are portraits of people of importance and of the servants of the house. The place is now occupied by several tenants, has suffered much from recent new construction, and in the rooms especially lacks most of its former grandeur.

House of the Marquesa de Uluapa. Detail of the main patio, looking toward the rear from the entre suelo or mezzaine level, showing the arches which support the main floor corridors. The stone of the apparently unsupported arches is so cut that the thrust carries through from wall to wall

Mexico City, Mexico, D. F.

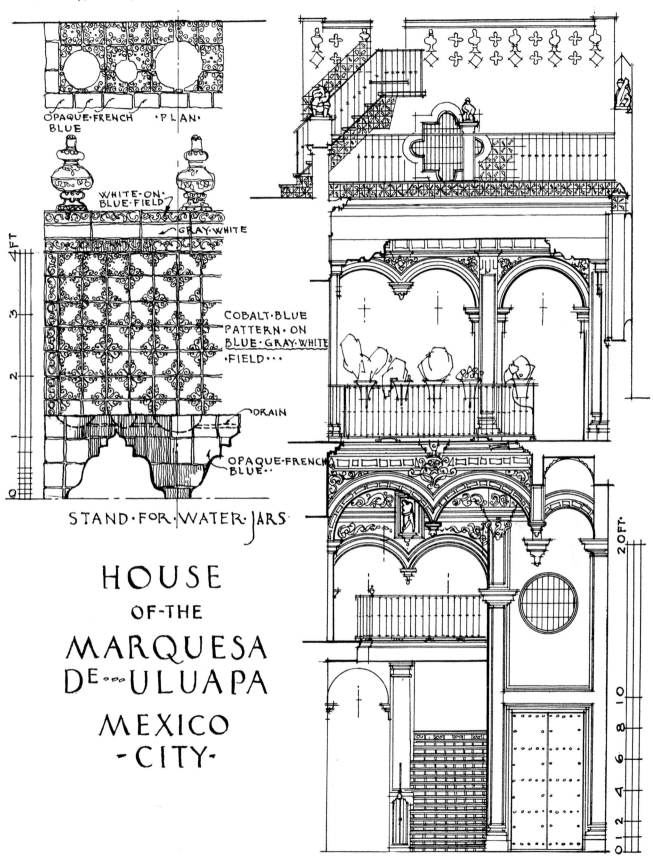

OPAQUE·FRENCH
BLUE   ·PLAN·

WHITE·ON·
BLUE·FIELD

GRAY·WHITE

COBALT·BLUE
PATTERN·ON
BLUE·GRAY·WHITE
·FIELD···

DRAIN

OPAQUE·FRENCH
BLUE··

STAND·FOR·WATER·JARS

HOUSE
OF·THE
MARQUESA
DE···ULUAPA
MEXICO
·CITY·

163

House of the Marquesa de Uluapa. A view from the landing of the stair which connects the entre suelo with the main floor. The stone treads and trimmer are carried on heavy open wood stringers set rather close together. Risers have glazed tile inserts. The finials are brass

House of the Marquesa de Uluapa. A view on the roof showing the railing around the patio and the mirador which is over the stair well. The miradors are a frequent feature of the Mexican house. From them a pleasant view is afforded. The construction above the railing of this one is modern

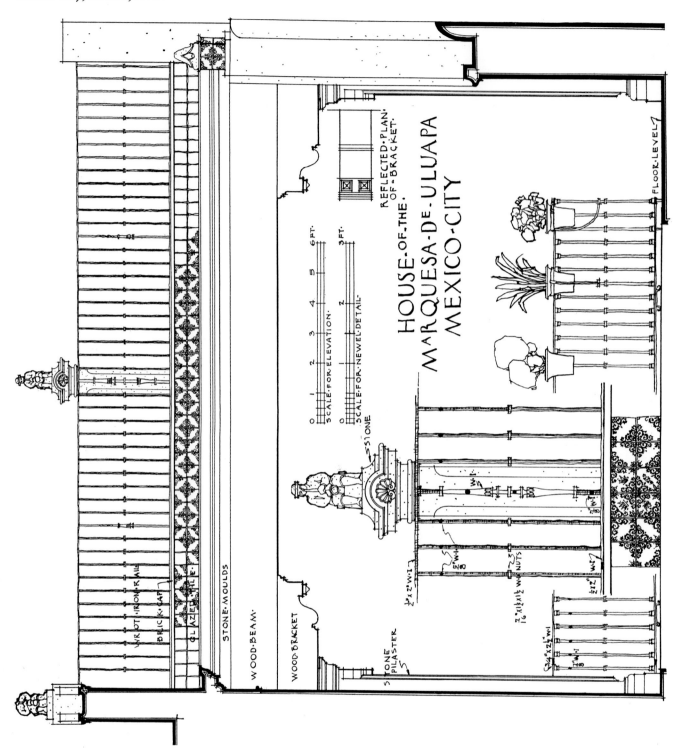

HOUSE·OF·THE·
MARQUESA·DE·ULUAPA
MEXICO·CITY

REFLECTED·PLAN·
OF·BRACKET·

SCALE·FOR·ELEVATION·

SCALE·FOR·NEWEL·DETAIL·

WROT·IRON·RAIL
BRICK·CAP
GLAZED·TILE
STONE·MOULDS
WOOD·BEAM·
WOOD·BRACKET
STONE·
PILASTER
FLOOR·LEVEL

Mexico City, Mexico, D. F.

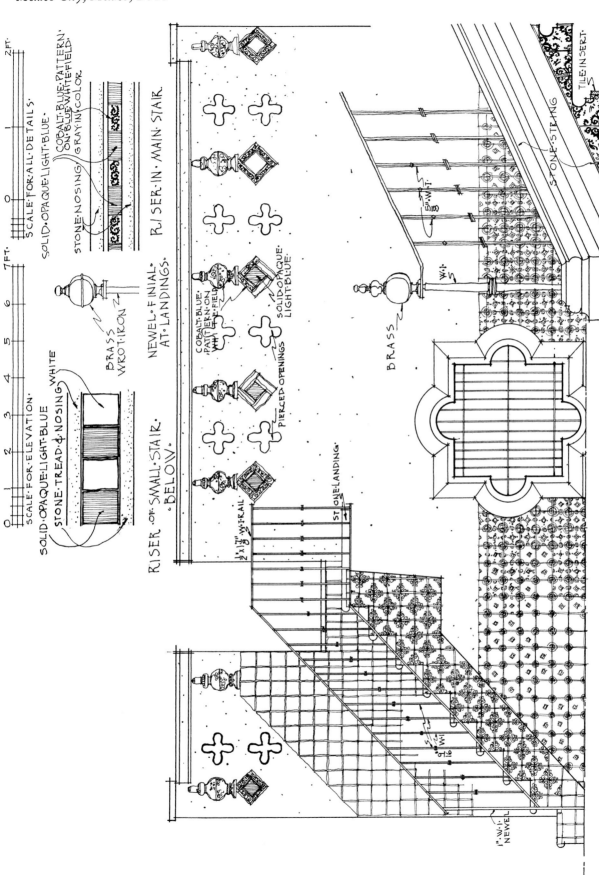

DETAIL·OF·MIRADOR·HOUSE·OF·THE·MARQUESA·DE·ULUAPA·

Mexico City, Mexico, D. F.

House of the Marquesa de Uluapa. A dado of blue and white glazed tile in one of the rooms. The floor is modern

House of the Marquesa de Uluapa. A niche for water jars. The tiles of the border and dado are blue and white. The ones above the top band are yellow, green, and black

House of the Marquesa de Uluapa. Blue and white glazed tile wainscot and stand for water jars in the open corridor of the main floor

House of the Marquesa de Uluapa. Stair in the second patio which leads from the main floor to the roof. The tiles are vari-colored. The wrought iron rail has a brass finial. The wood portion of the stair is new

House of the Marquesa de Uluapa. Looking up the stair well from the entre suelo level. This view shows the wood beams which support the stair and the blue and white tile inserts in the risers

Tacubaya, Mexico, D. F.

A small house at the Molino de Santo Domingo

THE END